A Year of
Knit Sweaters™

By Melissa Leapman

Editorial: Bobbie Matela, Kathy Wesley,
Mary Ann Frits, Sandy Scoville

Production: Deborah Michael, Amy S. Lin

Photography: Tammy Cromer-Campbell

We wish to thank Lion Brand Yarns for providing yarn.

Patterns tested and models made by Ellen Bray, Nancy Maakestad, Cheryl Marsolais, Eileen McNutt, JoAnn Moss, Sandy Scoville, Susie Adams Steele, Scarlet Taylor, Rita Weiss and Kathy Wesley.

©2003 by Melissa Leapman, published by American School of Needlework, Inc. The full line of ASN products is carried by Annie's Attic catalog.
TOLL-FREE ORDER LINE or to request a free catalog (800) 582-6643
Visit AnniesAttic.com.
Customer Service (800) 282-6643, fax (800) 882-6643

ISBN # 1-59012-065-5   Printed in U.S.A.   1 2 3 4 5 6 7 8 9

Introduction

Top knit designer Melissa Leapman created 12 terrific sweaters, most in sizes small to X-large, to keep your needles flying all year long. Melissa has perfected the art of shaping by using design techniques such as set-in sleeves and a variety of necklines. This attention to detail will add the look of professionalism to your knitting.

Directory

January

Color-Block Pullover

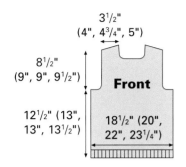

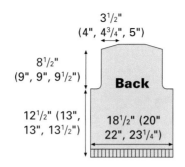

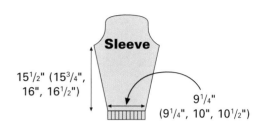

All measurements are approximate.

Sizes:

Small   Medium   Large   X-Large

Body Chest Measurement:
34"   36"   40"   42"

Garment Chest Measurement:
37"   40"   44"   46½"

Note: *Instructions are written for size small; changes for larger sizes are in parentheses.*

Materials:

Lion Brand Woolspun Thick & Thin, Dusty Mauve #141, Sage #123, Natural #098

For Size Small: 6 skeins Dusty Mauve, 2 skeins Sage, 1 skein Natural

For Size Medium: 7 skeins Dusty Mauve, 2 skeins Sage, 1 skein Natural

For Size Large: 7 skeins Dusty Mauve, 2 skeins Sage, 1 skein Natural

For Size X-Large: 8 skeins Dusty Mauve, 3 skeins Sage, 1 skein Natural

Size 11 (8mm) knitting needles, or size required for gauge

Size 11 (8mm) 16" circular knitting needle

Gauge:

In stockinette stitch (knit one row, purl one row):
3 sts = 1"

Instructions

Back

Ribbing:
With Sage, cast on 56 (60, 66, 70) sts.

Row 1 *(right side):*
* K1, P1; rep from * across.

Rep Row 1 until ribbing measures about 1½" from cast-on edge, ending by working a wrong side row.

Body:

Row 1 *(right side):*
Knit.

Row 2:
Purl.

Rows 3 through 8:
Rep Rows 1 and 2 three times more.

Row 9:
Rep Row 1.

Row 10:
With Natural, rep Row 2.

Rows 11 and 12:
With Natural, rep Rows 1 and 2.

With Dusty Mauve, rep Rows 1 and 2 until piece measures about 12½" (13", 13", 13½") from cast-on edge, ending by working a wrong side row.

Armhole Shaping:

Row 1 *(right side):*
Bind off 3 (3, 4, 5) sts; knit across—53 (57, 62, 65) sts.

Row 2:
Bind off 3 (3, 4, 5) sts; purl across—50 (54, 58, 60) sts.

Row 3:
Sl 1 as to knit, K1, PSSO; K46 (50, 54, 56); K2 tog—48 (52, 56, 58) sts.

Row 4:
P2 tog tbl; P44 (48, 52, 54); P2 tog—46 (50, 54, 56) sts.

Row 5:
Knit.

Row 6:
P2 tog tbl; P42 (46, 50, 52); P2 tog—44 (48, 52, 54) sts.

Row 7:
Knit.

Row 8:
P2 tog tbl; P40 (44, 48, 50); P2 tog—42 (46, 50, 52) sts.

For Size Small Only:

Work even (without dec) in stockinette st until piece measures about 20", ending by working a wrong side row.

Continue with Shoulder Shaping on page 6.

For Sizes Medium, Large, and X-Large Only:

Row 9:
Knit.

Row 10:
P2 tog tbl; P42 (46, 48); P2 tog—44 (48, 50) sts.

continued on page 6

Color-Block Pullover

Work even (without dec) in stockinette st until piece measures about 21" (21", 22"), ending by working a wrong side row.

Continue with Shoulder Shaping.

Shoulder Shaping (all sizes):

Row 1 *(right side):*
Bind off 5 (5, 6, 7) sts; knit across.

Row 2:
Bind off 5 (5, 6, 7) sts; purl across—32 (34, 36, 36) sts.

Row 3:
Bind off 5 (6, 7, 7) sts; knit across.

Row 4:
Bind off 5 (6, 7, 7) sts; purl across.

Bind off rem 22 sts.

Front

Work same as back until piece measures about 18¹/₂" (19¹/₂", 19¹/₂", 20¹/₂") from cast-on edge, and there are 6 rows less than back to shoulder shaping, ending by working a right side row.

Neck Shaping:

Row 1 *(wrong side):*
P16 (17, 19, 20); slip next 10 sts onto stitch holder; join second skein of yarn; P16 (17, 19, 20).

Row 2 *(right side):*
For left side, K16 (17, 19, 20); for right side, bind off 3 sts; K13 (14, 16, 17).

Row 3:
For right side, P13 (14, 16, 17); for left side, bind off 3 sts; P13 (14, 16, 17).

Row 4:
For left side, K13 (14, 16, 17); for right side, bind off 2 sts; K11 (12, 14, 15).

Row 5:
For right side, P11 (12, 14, 15); for left side, bind off 2 sts; P11 (12, 14, 15).

Shoulder Shaping:

Row 1 *(right side):*
On left shoulder, bind off 5 (5, 6, 7) sts; K4 (5, 6, 6), K2 tog; on right shoulder, sl 1, K1, PSSO; K9 (10, 12, 13).

Row 2:
On right shoulder, bind off 5 (5, 6, 7) sts; P5 (6, 7, 7); on left shoulder, P5 (6, 7, 7).

Row 3:
On left shoulder, bind off rem 5 (6, 7, 7) sts; on right shoulder, K5 (6, 7, 7).

Row 4:
On right shoulder, bind off rem 5 (6, 7, 7) sts.

Sleeve (make 2)

Ribbing:
With Sage, cast on 28 (28, 30, 32) sts.

Row 1 (right side):
* K1, P1; rep from * across.

Rep Row 1 until piece measures 1¹/₂" from cast-on edge.

Body:

Row 1 (right side):
Knit.

Row 2:
Purl.

Row 3:
Knit.

Row 4:
Inc (purl in front and back of next st); purl to last st; inc—30 (30, 32, 34) sts.

Rows 5 through 12:
Rep Rows 1 through 4 twice more. At end of Row 12—34 (34, 36, 38) sts.

Row 13:
With Natural, rep Row 1.

Row 14:
Rep Row 2.

Row 15:
Rep Row 1.

For Sizes Small, Large, and X-Large Only:

Row 16:
With Dusty Mauve, inc; purl to last st; inc—36 (38, 40) sts.

Row 17:
Knit.

Row 18:
Purl.

Rows 19 and 20:
Rep Rows 17 and 18 once more.

Row 21:
Knit.

Row 22:
Inc; purl to last st; inc—38 (40, 42) sts.

Rows 23 through 46 (58, 58):
Rep Rows 17 through 22 four (6, 6) times more. At end of Row 46 (58, 58)—46 (52, 54) sts.

Work even (without inc) until sleeve measures 15¹/₂" (16", 16¹/₂") from cast-on edge.

Shape Cap:

Row 1:
Bind off 3 (4, 5) sts; knit across.

Row 2:
Bind off 3 (4, 5) sts; purl across—40 (44, 44) sts.

Row 3:
Sl 1, K1, PSSO; knit to last 2 sts; K2 tog—38 (42, 42) sts.

Row 4:
P2 tog tbl; purl to last 2 sts; P2 tog—36 (40, 40) sts.

Rows 5 through 14 (16, 16):
Rep Rows 3 and 4 five (6, 6) times more. At end of Row 14 (16, 16)—16 (16, 16) sts.

Row 15 (17, 17):
Bind off 3 sts; knit across.

Row 16 (18, 18):
Bind off 3 sts; purl across—10 (10, 10) sts.

Rows 17 (19, 19) and 18 (20, 20):
Rep Rows 15 (17, 17) and 16 (18, 18).

Bind off rem 4 sts.

For Size Medium Only:

Row 16:
With Dusty Mauve, inc; purl to last st; inc—36 sts.

Rows 17 through 20:
Rep Rows 1 and 2 twice.

Row 21:
Rep Row 1.

Row 22:
Inc; purl to last st; inc—38 sts.

Rows 23 through 46:
Rep Rows 17 through 22 four times more. At end of Row 46—46 sts.

Work even (without inc) until sleeve measures about 15³/₄" from cast-on edge, ending by working a wrong side row.

Shape Cap:

Row 1 (right side):
Bind off 3 sts; knit across.

Row 2:
Bind off 3 sts; purl across—40 sts.

Row 3:
Knit.

Row 4:
P2 tog tbl; purl to last 2 sts; P2 tog—38 sts.

Rows 5 and 6:
Rep Rows 3 and 4. At end of Row 6—36 sts.

Row 7:
Sl 1, K1, PSSO; knit to last 2 sts; K2 tog.

Row 8:
P2 tog tbl; purl to last 2 sts; P2 tog.

Rows 9 through 16:
Rep Rows 7 and 8 four times more. At end of Row 16—16 sts.

Row 17:
Bind off 3 sts; knit across.

Row 18:
Bind off 3 sts; purl across.

Rows 19 and 20:
Rep Rows 17 and 18.

Bind off rem 4 sts.

Sew shoulder seams.

Neck Band

Hold sweater with right side facing you and right shoulder seam at top; with circular needle, pick up and knit 44 sts evenly spaced around neckline.

Rnd 1:
* K1, P1; rep from * around.

Rep Rnd 1 until neck band measures about 3¹/₂".

Bind off loosely in patt.

Finishing

Step 1:
Sew sleeves to body.

Step 2:
Sew sleeve and side seams.

Cabled Pullover with Rolled Edges

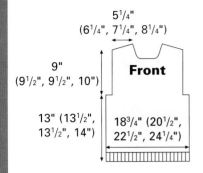

5¼"
(6¼", 7¼", 8¼")

9"
(9½", 9½", 10")
Front

13" (13½",
13½", 14")

18¾" (20½",
22½", 24¼")

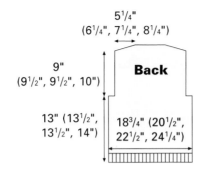

5¼"
(6¼", 7¼", 8¼")

9"
(9½", 9½", 10")
Back

13" (13½",
13½", 14")

18¾" (20½",
22½", 24¼")

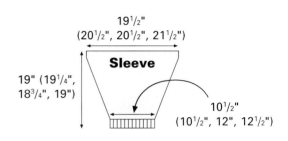

19½"
(20½", 20½", 21½")

Sleeve

19" (19¼",
18¾", 19")

10½"
(10½", 12", 12½")

All measurements are approximate.

Sizes:
Small   Medium   Large   X-Large

Body Chest Measurement:
34"   36"   40"   44"

Garment Chest Measurement:
37½"   41"   45"   48½"

Note: Instructions are written for size small; changes for larger sizes are in parentheses.

Materials:
Lion Brand Wool-Ease, Wheat #402
For Size Small: 9 skeins
For Size Medium: 9 skeins
For Size Large: 10 skeins
For Size X-Large: 11 skeins
Size 7 (4.5mm) knitting needles, or size required for gauge
Size 5 (3.75mm) knitting needles
Size 5 (3.75mm) 16" circular knitting needle
Cable needle

Gauge:
In stockinette stitch (knit one row, purl one row):
5 sts = 1"
In pattern:
6 sts = 1"

Pattern Stitches

Cable Back (CB):
Slip next 2 sts onto cable needle and hold in back of work, K2, K2 from cable needle—CB made.

Cable Front (CF):
Slip next 2 sts onto cable needle and hold in front of work, K2, K2 from cable needle—CF made.

Instructions

Back

Lower Edging:
With smaller size straight needles, cast on 104 (114, 124, 134) sts.

Row 1 *(right side)*:
Knit.

Row 2:
Purl.

Rows 3 through 6:
Rep Rows 1 and 2 twice more.

Row 7:
Rep Row 1.

Row 8:
Purl, inc (knit in front and back of next st) 18 (20, 22, 24) sts evenly spaced across row—122 (134, 146, 158) sts.

Ribbing:

Row 1 *(right side)*:
K2; ✱ P2, K2; rep from ✱ across.

Row 2:
P2; ✱ K2, P2; rep from ✱ across.

Rep Rows 1 and 2 until piece measures 2½" from cast-on edge, ending by working a wrong side row.

Change to larger size needles.

Body:

Row 1 *(right side)*:
Knit.

Row 2:
Purl.

Row 3:
K3; ✱ CB (see Pattern Stitches); CF (see Pattern Stitches); K4; rep from ✱ 8 (9, 10, 11) times more; CB; CF; K3.

Row 4:
Purl.

Row 5:
Knit.

Row 6:
Purl.

Row 7:
K1; ✱ CF; K4, CB; rep from ✱ 9 (10, 11, 12) times; K1.

Row 8:
Purl.

Rep Rows 1 through 8 until piece measures 13" (13½", 13½", 14") from cast-on edge, ending by working a wrong side row.

Armhole Shaping:

Row 1 *(right side)*:
Bind off 6 sts; work in patt across.

Row 2:
Rep Row 1. At end of row—110 (122, 134, 146) sts.

Continue in patt until piece measures 22" (23", 23", 24") from cast-on edge, ending by working a wrong side row.

   continued on page 10

Cabled Pullover With Rolled Edges

Shoulder Shaping:

Row 1:
Bind off 8 (9, 11, 12) sts; work in patt across.

Rows 2 through 4:
Rep Row 1. At end of Row 4—78 (86, 90, 98) sts.

Row 5:
Bind off 8 (10, 11, 13) sts; work in patt across.

Rows 6 through 8:
Rep Row 5.

Bind off rem 46 sts.

Front

Work same as back until piece measures about 20½" (21½", 21½", 22½") from cast-on edge, and there are 12 rows less than back to shoulder shaping, ending by working a wrong side row.

Neck and Shoulder Shaping:

Row 1 (right side):
Work in patt across first 43 (49, 55, 61) sts; join second skein of yarn; bind off next 24 sts; work in patt across rem 43 (49, 55, 61) sts.

Row 2:
Purl across both sides.

Row 3:
On left shoulder, work in patt across; on right shoulder, bind off 4 sts; work in patt across.

Row 4:
On right shoulder, work in patt across; on left shoulder, bind off 4 sts; work in patt across—39 (45, 51, 57) sts on each shoulder.

Row 5:
On left shoulder, work in patt across; on right shoulder, bind off 3 sts; work in patt across.

Row 6:
On right shoulder, work in patt across; on left shoulder, bind off 3 sts; work in patt across—36 (42, 48, 54) sts on each shoulder.

Row 7:
On left shoulder, work in patt across; on right shoulder, bind off 2 sts; work in patt across.

Row 8:
On right shoulder, work in patt across; on left shoulder, bind off 2 sts; work in patt across—34 (40, 46, 52) sts on each shoulder.

Row 9:
On left shoulder, bind off 8 (9, 11, 12) sts; work in patt to last 2 sts; K2 tog; on right shoulder, sl 1, K1, PSSO; work in patt across.

Row 10:
On right shoulder, bind off 8 (9, 11, 12) sts; work in patt to last 2 sts; P2 tog; on left shoulder, P2 tog tbl; work in patt across—24 (29, 33, 38) sts on each shoulder.

Row 11:
On left shoulder, bind off 8 (9, 11, 12) sts; on right shoulder, work in patt across.

Row 12:
On right shoulder, bind off 8 (9, 11, 12) sts—16 (20, 22, 26) sts on each shoulder.

Row 13:
On left shoulder, bind off 8 (10, 11, 13) sts; on right shoulder, work in patt across.

Row 14:
On right shoulder, bind off 8 (10, 11, 13) sts; on left shoulder, work in patt across—8 (10, 11, 13) sts.

Bind off rem sts.

Sleeve (make 2)

Rolled Edging:
With smaller size straight needles, cast on 52 (52, 62, 62) sts.

Row 1 (right side):
Knit.

Row 2:
Purl.

Rows 3 through 6:
Rep Rows 1 and 2 twice more.

Row 7:
Rep Row 1.

Row 8:
Inc (knit in front and back of next st) 10 (10, 12, 12) sts evenly spaced across row—62 (62, 74, 74) sts.

Ribbing:

Row 1 (right side):
K2; * P2, K2; rep from * across.

Row 2:
P2; * K2, P2; rep from * across. Rep Rows 1 and 2 until piece measures 2½" from cast-on edge, ending by working a wrong side row.

Change to larger size needles.

Body:

Row 1 (right side):
Inc (knit in front and back of next st); knit to last st; inc—64 (76) sts.

Row 2:
Purl.

Row 3:
Inc; K3; * CB (see Pattern Stitches on page 8); CF (see Pattern Stitches on page 8); K4; rep from * to last 12 sts; CB; CF; K3, inc—66 (78) sts.

Row 4:
Purl.

Row 5:
Inc; knit to last st; inc—68 (80) sts.

Row 6:
Purl.

Row 7:
Inc; K3; * CF; K4, CB; rep from * to last 4 sts; K3, inc—70 (82) sts.

Row 8:
Purl.

Row 9:
Knit.

Row 10:
Purl.

Row 11:
Inc; K6; * CB; CF; K4; rep from * to last 3 sts; K2, inc—72 (84) sts.

Rows 12 through 14:
Rep Rows 8 through 10.

Row 15:
Inc; K1, CB; CF; * K4, CB; CF; rep from * to last 2 sts; K1, inc—74 (86) sts.

Rows 16 through 18:
Rep Rows 8 through 10.

Row 19:
Inc; * CF; K4, CB; rep from * to last st; inc—76 (88) sts.

Rows 20 through 22:
Rep Rows 8 through 10.

Row 23:
Inc; K3, CB; CF; * K4, CB; CF; rep from * to last 4 sts; K3, inc—78 (90) sts.

Rows 24 through 26:
Rep Rows 8 through 10.

Row 27:
Inc; K2; * CF; K4, CB; rep from * to last 3 sts; K2, inc—80 (92) sts.

Rows 28 through 30:
Rep Rows 8 through 10.

Row 31:
Inc; K5, CB, CF; * K4, CB; CF; rep from * to last 6 sts; K5, inc—82 (94) sts.

Rows 32 through 34:
Rep Rows 8 through 10.

Row 35:
Inc; CB; CF; * K4, CB; CF; rep from * to last st; inc—84 (96) sts.

Rows 36 through 38:
Rep Rows 8 through 10.

Row 39:
Inc; K7; CB; CF; * K4, CB; CF; rep from * to last 8 sts; K7, inc—86 (98) sts.

Rows 40 through 42:
Rep Rows 8 through 10.

Row 43:
Inc; K2; * CB; CF; K4; rep from * to last 11 sts; CB; CF; K2, inc—88 (100) sts.

Rows 44 through 46:
Rep Rows 8 through 10.

Row 47:
Inc; K1; * CF; K4, CB; rep from * to last 3 sts; K1, inc—90 (102) sts.

Rows 48 through 50:
Rep Rows 8 through 10.

Row 51:
Inc; K4; * CB; CF; K4; rep from * to last st; inc—92 (104) sts.

Rows 52 through 54:
Rep Rows 8 through 10.

Row 55:
Inc; K3; * CF; K4, CB; rep from * to last 4 sts; K3, inc—94 (106) sts.

Rows 56 through 58:
Rep Rows 8 through 10.

Rows 59 through 106:
Rep Rows 11 through 58. At end of Row 106—118 (130) sts.

Work even in patt until sleeve measures about 19" (19") from cast-on edge, ending by working a right side row.

Bind off.

For Size Medium Only:

Row 1 (right side):
Inc (knit in front and back of next st); K60; inc—64 sts.

Row 2:
Purl.

Row 3:
Inc; K3; * CB (see Pattern Stitches on page 8); CF (see Pattern Stitches on page 8); K4; rep from * 3 times more; CB; CF; K3, inc—66 sts.

Row 4:
Purl.

Row 5:
Inc; K64; inc—68 sts.

Row 6:
Purl.

Row 7:
Inc; K3; * CF; K4, CB; rep from * 4 times more; K3, inc—70 sts.

Row 8:
Purl.

Row 9:
Inc; K68; inc—72 sts.

Row 10:
Purl.

Row 11:
Inc; K7; * CB; CF; K4; rep from * to last 4 sts; K3, inc—74 sts.

Row 12:
Purl.

Rows 13 through 68:
Rep Rows 1 through 58 of Sizes Small and X-Large. At end of Row 68—106 sts.

Rows 69 through 104:
Rep Rows 11 through 46 of Sizes Small and X-Large. At end of Row 104—124 sts.

Work even in patt (without inc) until sleeve measures about 19 1/4" from cast-on edge, ending by working a right side row.

Bind off.

For Size Large Only:

Row 1 (right side):
Knit.

Row 2:
Purl.

Rows 3 through 22:
Rep Rows 43 through 58 of Sizes Small and X-Large. At end of Row 22—82 sts.

Rows 23 through 70:
Rep Rows 11 through 58 of Sizes Small and X-Large. At end of Row 70—106 sts.

Rows 71 through 106:
Rep Rows 11 through 46 of Sizes Small and X-Large. At end of Row 106—124 sts.

Work even in patt (without inc) until sleeve measures about 18¾" from cast-on edge, ending by working a right side row.

Bind off.

Sew shoulder seams.

Neck Ribbing
Hold sweater with right side facing you and right shoulder seam at top; with circular needle, pick up and knit 92 sts evenly spaced around neckline.

Rnd 1:
* K2, P2; rep from * around.

Rep Rnd 1 until ribbing measures about 3" from cast-on edge.

Rolled Edging:
Rnd 1:
K5, K2 tog; * K8, K2 tog; rep from * 7 times more; K5—83 sts.

Rnds 2 through 8:
Knit.

Bind off loosely.

Finishing
Step 1:
Referring to diagram, sew sleeves to body.

Step 2:
Sew sleeve and side seams.

Weekend Classic Pullover

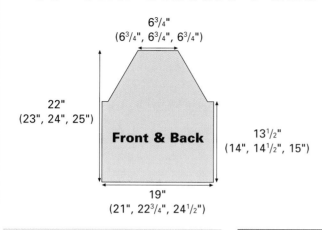

6³/₄"
(6³/₄", 6³/₄", 6³/₄")

22"
(23", 24", 25")

Front & Back

13¹/₂"
(14", 14¹/₂", 15")

19"
(21", 22³/₄", 24¹/₂")

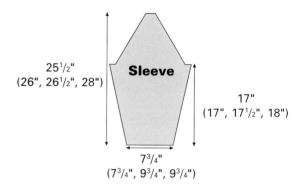

25¹/₂"
(26", 26¹/₂", 28")

Sleeve

17"
(17", 17¹/₂", 18")

7³/₄"
(7³/₄", 9³/₄", 9³/₄")

All measurements are approximate.

Sizes:
Small   Medium   Large   X-Large

Body Chest Measurement:
32"   36"   38"   42"

Garment Chest Measurement:
38"   42"   45¹/₂"   49"

Note: Instructions are written for size small; changes for larger sizes are in parentheses.

Materials:
Lion Brand Wool-Ease
Sportweight, Green Heather #30
For Size Small: 4 skeins
For Size Medium: 5 skeins
For Size Large: 5 skeins
for Size X-Large: 6 skeins
Size 5 (3.75mm) straight knitting
   needles, or size required for gauge
Size 5 (3.75mm) 16" circular knitting
   needle
Markers
Four stitch holders

Gauge:
In stockinette stitch (knit one row, purl one row):
5 sts = 1"
In pattern:
30 sts = 4"

Special Abbreviations

Slip, Slip, Knit (SSK):
Slip next 2 sts, one at a time, as to knit **(Fig 1)**; insert left-hand needle through both sts from left to right **(Fig 2)**; K2 tog—SSK made.

Fig 1

Fig 2

Slip, Slip, Purl (SSP):
Slip next 2 sts one at a time, as to knit; slip these 2 sts back onto left-hand needle **(Fig 1)**; P2 tog tbl **(Fig 2)**—SSP made.

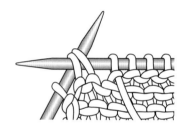

Fig 1

Fig 2

Instructions

Back/Front (make 2)
With straight needles, cast on 143 (157, 171, 185) sts.

Row 1 *(right side):*
K1, P1, K1; * P1, K2, (P1, K1) twice; rep from * across.

Row 2:
K1, P1; * K2, P2, K2, P1; rep from * to last st; K1.

Rep Rows 1 and 2 until piece measures 13¹/₂" (14", 14¹/₂", 15") from cast-on edge, ending by working a wrong side row.

Armhole Shaping:
Row 1 *(right side):*
Bind off 4 sts; work in patt across.

Row 2:
Rep Row 1—135 (149, 163, 177) sts.

Row 3:
K1, SSK (see Special Abbreviations); work in patt to last 3 sts; K2 tog; K1— 133 (147, 161, 175) sts.

continued on page 14

Weekend Classic Pullover

Row 4:
Work in patt across.

Rows 5 through 70 (64, 62, 56):
Rep Rows 3 and 4, 33 (30, 29, 26) times more. At end of last row—67 (87, 103, 123) sts.

Row 71 (65, 63, 57):
Rep Row 3—65 (85, 101, 121) sts.

Row 72 (66, 64, 58):
P1, P2 tog; work in patt to last 3 sts; SSP (see Special Abbreviations on page 12); P1—63 (83, 99, 119).

Rows 73 (67, 65, 59) through 78 (82, 88, 92):
Rep last 2 rows 3 (8, 12, 17) times more. At end of last row—51 sts. Slip these sts onto a stitch holder.

Sleeve (make 2)
With straight needles, cast on 59 (59, 73, 73) sts.

Row 1 (right side):
K1, P1, K1; * P1, K2, (P1, K1) twice; rep from * across.

Row 2:
K1, P1; * K2, P2, K2, P1; rep from * to last st; K1.

Rows 3 and 4:
Rep Rows 1 and 2.

Row 5:
Rep Row 1.

Row 6:
Inc (knit in front and back of next st); P1; * K2, P2, K2, P1; rep from * to last st; inc—61 (61, 75, 75) sts.

Row 7:
(P1, K1) twice; * P1, K2, (P1, K1) twice; rep from * to last st; P1.

Row 8:
K2, P1; * K2, P2, K2, P1; rep from * to last 2 sts; K2.

Rows 9 and 10:
Rep Rows 7 and 8 once.

Row 11:
Rep Row 7.

Row 12:
Inc; K1, P1; * K2, P2, K2, P1; rep from * to last 2 sts; K1, inc—63 (63, 77, 77) sts.

Continue working in patt, inc each end every 6th row 20 (20, 14, 20) times more, then each end every 8th row 1 (1, 6, 2) time(s). At end of last row—105 (105, 117, 121) sts.

Work even (without inc) until sleeve measures 17" (17", 17½", 18") from cast-on edge, ending by working a wrong side row.

Cap Shaping:

Row 1 *(right side):*
Bind off 4 sts; work in patt across.

Row 2:
Rep Row 1—97 (97, 109, 113) sts.

Row 3:
K1, SSK (see Special Abbreviations on page 12); work in patt to last 3 sts; K2 tog; K1—95 (95, 107, 111) sts.

Row 4:
Work in patt across.

Rows 5 through 66 (74, 74, 78):
Rep Rows 3 and 4, (31, 35, 35, 37) times more. At end of last row—33 (25, 37, 37) sts.

Row 67 (75, 75, 79):
Rep Row 3—31 (23, 35, 35) sts.

Row 68 (76, 76, 80):
P1, P2 tog; work in patt to last 3 sts; SSP (see Special Abbreviations on page 12); P1—29 (21, 33, 33) sts.

Rows 69 (77, 77, 81) through 80 (84, 90, 94):
Rep last 2 rows 5 (3, 6, 6) times more. At end of last row—9 sts.

Slip these sts onto a stitch holder.

With right sides facing you, sew sleeves to body.

Neck Band

Hold sweater with right side facing you; beg at left sleeve, slip sts from stitch holders onto circular needle—120 sts.

Rnd 1:
* K2 tog; work in patt over next 5 sts; SSK; on body, K2 tog; work in patt over next 47 sts; SSK; rep from * once more—112 sts.

Rnd 2:
* K2, (P1, K1) twice; P1; rep from * around.

Rnd 3:
* K2, P2, K1, P2; rep from * around.

Rep Rnds 2 and 3 until neck band measures 6½" from beg.

Bind off loosely.

Finishing

Step 1:
Sew sleeve and side seams, leaving lower 3" (4", 4", 4½") of sides open.

Step 2:
Fold neck band in half to wrong side. Sew in place.

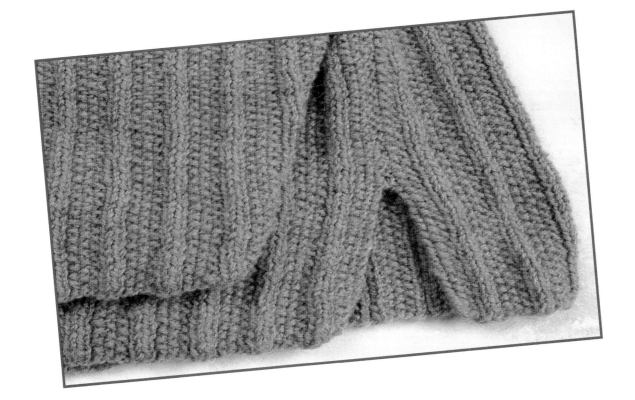

Chenille Pullover

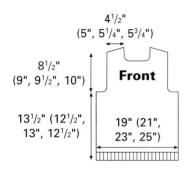

Front

4¹/₂"
(5", 5¹/₄", 5³/₄")

8¹/₂"
(9", 9¹/₂", 10")

13¹/₂" (12¹/₂",
13", 12¹/₂")

19" (21",
23", 25")

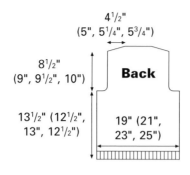

Back

4¹/₂"
(5", 5¹/₄", 5³/₄")

8¹/₂"
(9", 9¹/₂", 10")

13¹/₂" (12¹/₂",
13", 12¹/₂")

19" (21",
23", 25")

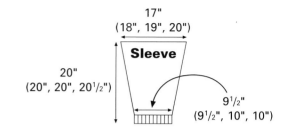

Sleeve

17"
(18", 19", 20")

20"
(20", 20", 20¹/₂")

9¹/₂"
(9¹/₂", 10", 10")

All measurements are approximate.

Sizes:
Small   Medium   Large   X-Large

Body Chest Measurement:
32"   36"   38"   42"

Garment Chest Measurement:
38"   42"   46"   50"

Note: *Instructions are written for size small; changes for larger sizes are in parentheses.*

Materials:
Lion Brand Chenille Sensations, Antique White #089, Sage #173, Violet #145, and Denim Blue #111
For Size Small: 11 skeins Antique White; 2 skeins Sage; 1 skein each Violet and Denim Blue
For Size Medium: 11 skeins Antique White; 2 skeins Sage; 1 skein each Violet and Denim Blue
For Size Large: 14 skeins Antique White; 2 skeins Sage; 1 skein each Violet and Denim Blue
For Size X-Large: 15 skeins Antique White; 2 skeins Sage; 1 skein each Violet and Denim Blue
Size 7 (4.5mm) straight knitting needles, or size required for gauge
Size 7 (4.5mm) 16" circular knitting needle
Markers
Two stitch holders

Gauge:
In stockinette stitch (knit one row, purl one row):
4 sts = 1"

Instructions
Notes: *When working from chart in rows, read right side rows from right to left, and wrong side rows from left to right. When changing color, bring new color under old color, twisting to prevent holes. Move markers as you come to them.*

Back
With straight needles and Antique White, cast on 77 **(85, 93, 101)** sts.

Ribbing:
Row 1 *(right side)*:
K1, P1; rep from * across.

Rep Row 1 until ribbing measures about 2" **(2", 3", 3")** from cast-on edge, ending by working a wrong side row.

Body:
Row 1 *(right side)*:
K30 **(34, 38, 42)**; place marker, K17; place marker, K30 **(34, 38, 42)**.

Row 2:
P30 **(34, 38, 42)**; P17, K30 **(34, 38, 42)**.

Rows 3 through 6:
Rep Rows 1 and 2 twice more.

Row 7:
K30 **(34, 38, 42)**; with Violet, K17 (see Row 7 of Chart A on page 18); join second skein of Antique White, K30 **(34, 38, 42)**.

Row 8:
P30 **(34, 38, 42)**; from Chart A, with Violet, P17; with Antique White, P30 **(34, 38, 42)**.

Continue in stockinette st (knit one row, purl one row), working center 17 sts from Chart A beginning on Row 9, and continuing until piece measures 13" **(12¹/₂", 13", 12¹/₂")** from cast-on edge, ending by working a wrong side row.

Armhole Shaping:
Row 1 *(right side)*:
Bind off 6 **(8, 10, 12)** sts; knit across working 17 center sts on next row of Chart A.

continued on page 18

Chart A

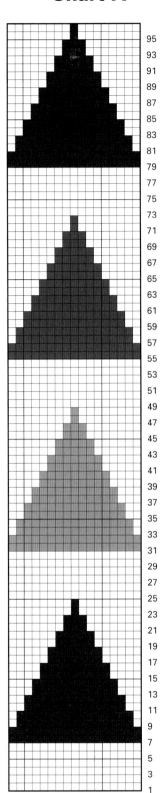

Middle 17 sts

□ Antique White
■ Violet
▦ Sage
▨ Denim Blue

Row 2:
Bind off 6 (8, 10, 12) sts; purl across working 17 center sts on next row of Chart A— 65 (69, 73, 77) sts.

Rows 3 through 96:
Continue in stockinette st, working center 17 sts from Chart A. After working Row 96 of Chart A, repeat Rows 25 through 48 once.

Continue in stockinette st with Antique White only until piece measures about 21½" (21½", 22½", 22½") from cast-on edge, ending by working a wrong side row.

Shoulder Shaping:

Row 1 *(right side):*
Bind off 6 (7, 7, 8) sts; knit across.

Row 2:
Bind off 6 (7, 7, 8) sts; purl across.

Rows 3 and 4:
Rep Rows 1 and 2.

Row 5:
Bind off 6 (6, 7, 7) sts; knit across.

Row 6:
Bind off 6 (6, 7, 7) sts; purl across.

Slip rem 29 (29, 31, 31) sts onto stitch holder for back of neck.

Front
Work same as for Back through Row 2 of Armhole Shaping.

Continue in stockinette st, working center 17 sts from Chart A.

Continue in stockinette st with Antique White only to Shoulder Shaping, ending by working a wrong side row.

Neck Shaping:

Row 1 *(right side):*
K25 (27, 28, 30); slip next 15 (15, 17, 17) sts onto stitch holder; join second skein of Antique White; K25 (27, 28, 30).
Note: *Work across both shoulders at same time with separate skeins of yarn.*

Row 2:
Purl.

Row 3:
On left shoulder, knit across; on right shoulder, bind off next 3 sts; knit across.

Row 4:
On right shoulder, purl across; on left shoulder, bind off 3 sts; purl across— 22 (24, 25, 27) sts on each shoulder.

Row 5:
On left shoulder, knit across; on right shoulder, bind off 3 sts; knit across.

Row 6:
On right shoulder, purl across; on left shoulder, bind off 3 sts; purl across— 19 (21, 22, 24) sts on each shoulder.

Row 7:
On left shoulder, K16 (18, 19, 21), K2 tog; K1; on right shoulder, K1, SSK; K16 (18, 19, 21)—18 (20, 21, 23) sts on each shoulder.

Row 8:
Purl across both shoulders.

Shoulder Shaping:

Row 1:
Bind off 6 (7, 7, 8) sts; knit across both shoulders.

Row 2:
Bind off 6 (7, 7, 8) sts; purl across both shoulders.

Rows 3 and 4:
Rep Rows 1 and 2.

Row 5:
Bind off 6 (6, 7, 7) sts; knit across.

Row 6:
Bind off rem 6 (6, 7, 7) sts.

Sleeve (make 2)

Ribbing:

With straight needles and Antique White, cast on 38 (38, 40, 40) sts.

Row 1 *(right side):*
* K1, P1; rep from * across.

Rep Row 1 until piece measures 2" from cast-on edge.

Body:

Row 1 *(right side):*
Knit.

Row 2:
Purl.

Row 3:
Inc (knit in front and back of next st); knit to last st; inc—40 (40, 42, 42) sts.

Row 4:
Purl.

Rows 5 through 12 (40, 56, 80):
Rep Rows 1 through 4 two (9, 13, 19) times more. At end of last row—44 (58, 68, 80) sts.

For Sizes Small, Medium, and Large Only:

Rows 13 (41, 57) through 16 (44, 60):
Rep Rows 1 and 2 twice more.

Rows 17 (45, 61) and 18 (46, 62):
Rep Rows 3 and 4. At end of last row—46 (60, 70) sts.

Rows 19 (47, 63) through 84 (82, 80):
Rep Rows 13 (41, 57) through 18 (46, 62) eleven (6, 3) times more. At end of last row—68 (72, 76) sts.

Continue with For All Sizes below.

For Size X-Large Only:

Continue with For All Sizes.

For All Sizes

Continue in stockinette st (knit one row, purl one row) until sleeve measures 20" (20", 20", 20½") from cast-on edge.

Bind off.

Sew shoulder seams.

Neck Band

Hold sweater with right side facing you and right shoulder at top; with circular needle and Antique White, knit 29 (29, 31, 31) sts from back stitch holder; pick up and knit 12 (12, 12, 12) sts along left front shoulder; knit 15 (15, 17, 17) sts from front stitch holder; pick up and knit 12 (12, 12, 12) sts along right front shoulder—68 (68, 72, 72) sts.

Rnd 1:
Knit.

Rnds 2 through 8:
Rep Rnd 1.

Bind off loosely allowing neck band to roll forward.

Finishing

Step 1:
Referring to diagram, sew sleeves to body.

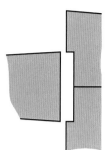

Step 2:
Sew sleeve and side seams.

Cables 'n' Ribs Turtleneck

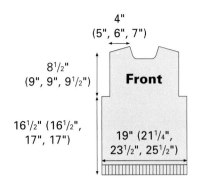

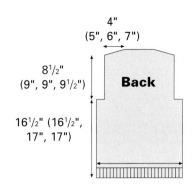

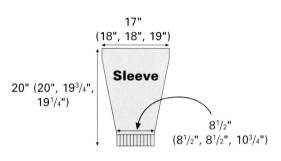

All measurements are approximate.

Sizes:
Small   Medium   Large   X-Large

Body Chest Measurement:
32"   36"   40"   44"

Garment Chest Measurement:
38"   42½"   47"   51"
Note: Instructions are written for size small; changes for larger sizes are in parentheses.

Materials:
Lion Brand Imagine, Pink #101
For Size Small: 9 skeins
For Size Medium: 9 skeins
For Size Large: 10 skeins
For Size X-Large: 10 skeins
Size 7 (4.5mm) knitting needles
Size 9 (5.5mm) knitting needles, or size required for gauge
Size 7 (4.5mm) 16" circular knitting needle
Cable needle

Gauge:
In stockinette stitch (knit one row, purl one row):
17 sts = 4"

Pattern Stitches

Cable Back (CB):
Slip next 3 sts onto cable needle and hold in back of work, K3, K3 from cable needle—CB made.

Cable Front (CF):
Slip next 3 sts onto cable needle and hold in front of work, K3, K3 from cable needle—CF made.

Instructions

Back
With smaller size needles, cast on 163 (181, 199, 217) sts.

Ribbing:

Row 1 *(right side):*
K2; * P3, K3; rep from * 25 (28, 31, 34) times more; P3, K2.

Row 2:
P2; * K3, P3; rep from * 25 (28, 31, 34) times more; K3, P2.

Rep Rows 1 and 2 until ribbing measures 2" from cast-on edge, ending by working a wrong side row.

Change to larger size needles.

Body:

Row 1 *(right side):*
K2; * P3, K9, P3, K3; rep from * 7 (8, 9, 10) times more; P3, K9, P3, K2.

Row 2:
P2; * K3, P9, K3, P3; rep from * 7 (8, 9, 10) times more; P9, K3, P2.

Row 3:
K2, P3, K3; * CB (see Pattern Stitches); (P3, K3) twice; rep from * 7 (8, 9, 10) times more; CB; P3, K2.

Row 4:
Rep Row 2.

Row 5:
Rep Row 1.

Row 6:
Rep Row 2.

Row 7:
K2; * P3, CF (see Pattern Stitches); K3, P3, K3; rep from * 7 (8, 9, 10) times more; P3, CF; K3, P3, K2.

Row 8:
Rep Row 2.

Rep Rows 1 through 8 until piece measures about 16½" (16½", 17", 17") from cast-on edge, ending by working a wrong side row.

Armhole Shaping:

Row 1 *(right side):*
Bind off 16 sts; work in patt across.

Row 2:
Rep Row 1. At end of row—131 (149, 167, 185) sts.

Continue in patt until piece measures 25" (25½", 26", 26½") from cast-on edge, ending by working a wrong side row.

Shoulder Shaping:

Row 1 *(right side):*
Bind off 12 (15, 18, 21) sts; work in patt across.

Rows 2 through 6:
Rep Row 1. At end of Row 6—59 sts.

Bind off.

 continued on page 22

Cables 'n' Ribs Turtleneck

Front

Work same as Back until there are 10 rows less than back to shoulder shaping, ending by working a wrong side row.

Neck and Shoulder Shaping:

Row 1 (*right side*):
Work in patt across first 53 (62, 71, 80) sts; join second skein of yarn; bind off next 25 sts; work in patt across rem sts.

Row 2:
Work in patt across both sides.

Row 3:
On left shoulder, work in patt across; on right shoulder, bind off 8 sts; work in patt across.

Row 4:
On right shoulder, work in patt across; on left shoulder, bind off 8 sts; work in patt across—45 (54, 63, 72) sts on each shoulder.

Row 5:
On left shoulder, work in patt across; on right shoulder, bind off 5 sts; work in patt across.

Row 6:
On right shoulder, work in patt across; on left shoulder, bind off 5 sts; work in patt across—40 (49, 58, 67) sts on each shoulder.

Row 7:
On left shoulder, work in patt to last 2 sts; K2 tog; on right shoulder, sl 1 as to knit, K1, PSSO; work in patt across.

Row 8:
On right shoulder, work in patt to last 2 sts; P2 tog tbl; on left shoulder, P2 tog; work in patt across.

Rows 9 and 10:
Rep Rows 7 and 8. At end of Row 10— 36 (45, 54, 63) sts on each shoulder.

Row 11:
Bind off 12 (15, 18, 21) sts; work in patt across both shoulders.

Rows 12 through 15:
Rep Row 11.

Bind off rem sts.

Sleeve (make 2)
With smaller size needles, cast on 73 (73, 73, 91) sts.

Ribbing:

Row 1 (*right side*):
K2; * P3, K3; rep from * 10 (10, 10, 13) times more; P3, K2.

Row 2:
P2; * K3, P3; rep from * 10 (10, 10, 13) times more; K3, P2.

Rep Rows 1 and 2 until ribbing measures 2" from cast-on edge, ending by working a wrong side row.

Change to larger size needles.

Body:

Row 1 (right side):
K2; * P3, K9, P3, K3; rep from * 2 (2, 2, 3) times more; P3, K9, P3, K2.

Row 2:
P2; * K3, P9, K3, P3; rep from * 2 (2, 2, 3) times more; K3, P9, K3, P2.

Row 3:
Inc (knit in front and back of next st); K1, P3, K3; * CB (see Pattern Stitches on page 20); (P3, K3) twice; rep from * 2 (2, 2, 3) times more; CB; P3, K1, inc—75 (75, 75, 93) sts.

Row 4:
P3, K3; * P9, K3, P3, K3; rep from * 2 (2, 2, 3) times more; P9, K3, P3.

Row 13:
Inc; P3, K3, P3; * K9, P3, K3, P3; rep from * 3 (3, 3, 4) times more; inc—85 (85, 85, 103) sts.

Row 14:
P2, K3, P3, K3; * P9, K3, P3, K3; rep from * 3 (3, 3, 4) times more; P2.

Row 15:
Inc; K1, P3; * K3, P3, CF; K3, P3; rep from * 3 (3, 3, 4) times more; K3, P3, K1, inc—87 (87, 87, 105) sts.

Row 16:
(P3, K3) twice; * P9, K3, P3, K3; rep from * 3 (3, 3, 4) times more; P3.

Continue in patt, inc one st each end every right side row 18 (28, 29, 20) times more, then every 4th row 10 (5, 4, 8) times. At end of last row—143 (153, 153, 161) sts.

Work even (without inc) until sleeve measures 20" (20", 19³/₄", 19¹/₄"), ending by working a right side row.

Bind off.

Sew shoulder seams.

Neck Ribbing
Hold sweater with right side facing you and right shoulder seam at top; with circular needle, pick up and knit 78 sts around neckline.

Rnd 1:
* K3, P3; rep from * around.

Rep Rnd 1 until neck ribbing measures 8".

Bind off loosely in patt.

Finishing
Step 1:
Referring to diagram, sew sleeves to body.

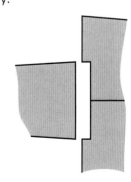

Step 2:
Sew sleeve and side seams.

Row 5:
Inc; K2; * P3, K9, P3, K3; rep from * 2 (2, 2, 3) times more; P3, K9, P3, K2, inc—77 (77, 77, 95) sts.

Row 6:
K1, P3; * K3, P9, K3, P3; rep from * 3 (3, 3, 4) times more; K1.

Row 7:
Inc; K3; * P3, CF (see Pattern Stitches on page 20); K3, P3, K3; rep from * 3 (3, 3, 4) times more; inc—79 (79, 79, 97) sts.

Row 8:
K2, P3; * K3, P9, K3, P3; rep from * 3 (3, 3, 4) times more; K2.

Row 9:
Inc; P1, K3; * P3, K9, P3, K3; rep from * 3 (3, 3, 4) times more; P1, inc—81 (81, 81, 99) sts.

Row 10:
K3, P3, K3; * P9, K3, P3, K3; rep from * 3 (3, 3, 4) times more.

Row 11:
Inc; P2, K3; * P3, K3, CB; P3, K3; rep from * 3 (3, 3, 4) times more; P2, inc—83 (83, 83, 101) sts.

Row 12:
P1, K3, P3, K3; * P9, K3, P3, K3; rep from * 3 (3, 3, 4) times more; P1.

Textured Jacket

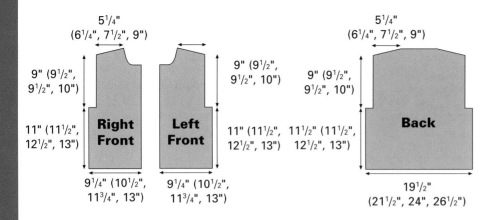

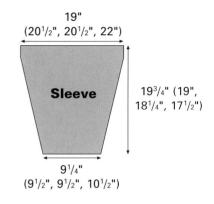

All measurements are approximate.

Sizes:

Small   Medium   Large   X-Large

Body Chest Measurement:
32"   36"   40"   44"

Garment Chest Measurement:
38"   43"   48"   53"

Note: Instructions are written for size small; changes for larger sizes are in parentheses.

Materials:

Lion Brand Homespun,
    Barrington #336
For Size Small: 5 skeins
For Size Medium: 6 skeins
For Size Large: 6 skeins
For Size X-Large: 7 skeins
Size 10 (6mm) knitting needles,
    or size required for gauge
Size K (10.5mm) crochet hook
One button, 1"-diameter
Sewing needle and matching thread

Gauge:

In stockinette stitch (knit one row, purl one row):
7 sts = 2"

Instructions

Back

Body:
Cast on 62 (70, 78, 86) sts.

Row 1 *(right side)*:
K2; * P2, K2; rep from * across.

Row 2:
P2; * K2, P2; rep from * across.

Row 3:
Rep Row 2.

Row 4:
Rep Row 1.
Rep Rows 1 through 4 until piece measures about 11" (11½", 12½", 13") from cast-on edge, ending by working a Row 4.

Armhole Shaping:

Row 1 *(right side)*:
Bind off 4 sts; K2; * P2, K2; rep from * across—58 (66, 74, 82) sts.

Row 2:
Bind off 4 sts; P2; * K2, P2; rep from * across—54 (62, 70, 78) sts.

Row 3:
P2; * K2, P2; rep from * across.

Row 4:
K2; * P2, K2; rep from * across.

Row 5:
Rep Row 4.

Row 6:
Rep Row 3.

Rep Rows 3 through 6 until piece measures about 20" (21", 22", 23") from cast-on edge, ending by working a wrong side row.

Shoulder Shaping:

Row 1 *(right side)*:
Bind off 5 (6, 8, 9) sts; work in patt across—49 (56, 62, 73) sts.

Rows 2 through 4:
Rep Row 1. At end of Row 4—34 (38, 38, 42) sts.

Row 5:
Bind off 6 (7, 7, 9) sts; work in patt across—28 (31, 31, 33) sts.

Row 6:
Rep Row 5—22 (24, 24, 24) sts.

Bind off rem sts.

Left Front
Cast on 30 (34, 38, 42) sts.

Row 1 *(right side)*:
K2; * P2, K2; rep from * across.

Row 2:
P2; * K2, P2; rep from * across.

Row 3:
Rep Row 2.

Row 4:
Rep Row 1.

Rep Rows 1 through 4 until piece measures same as Back to armhole shaping.

Armhole Shaping:

Row 1 *(right side)*:
Bind off 4 sts; work in patt across—26 (30, 34, 38) sts.

continued on page 26

Textured Jacket

Continue in patt until piece measures about 18½" (19½", 20½", 21½") from cast-on edge, ending by working a right side row.

Neck Shaping:

Row 1 *(wrong side)*:
Bind off 4 sts; work in patt across—22 (26, 30, 34) sts.

Row 2 *(right side)*:
Work in patt across.

Row 3:
Bind off 2 sts; work in patt across—20 (24, 28, 32) sts.

Row 4:
Work in patt across.

Row 5:
K1, P2 tog tbl; work in patt across.

Row 6:
Work in patt to last 3 sts; K2 tog; K1.

Continuing in patt, dec one st on neck edge 4 (5, 5, 5) times; AT THE SAME TIME, when piece measures same as back to shoulder shaping, on right side rows, bind off 5 (6, 8, 9) sts twice, then bind off rem 6 (7, 7, 9) sts.

Right Front

Cast on 30 (34, 38, 42) sts.

Row 1 *(right side)*:
K2; * P2, K2; rep from * across.

Row 2:
P2; * K2, P2; rep from * across.

Row 3:
Rep Row 2.

Row 4:
Rep Row 1.

Rep Rows 1 through 4 until piece measures same as back to Armhole Shaping, ending by working a right side row.

Armhole Shaping:

Row 1 *(wrong side)*:
Bind off 4 sts; work in patt across—26 (30, 34, 38) sts.

Continue in patt until piece measures 2 rows less than Left Front to neck shaping, ending by working a wrong side row.

Next Row *(right side)*:
Work patt across first 2 sts; for buttonhole, bind off next 2 sts; work in patt across.

Next Row:
Work in patt to bound-off sts; cast on 2 sts; work rem sts in patt.

Neck Shaping:

Row 1 *(right side)*:
Bind off 4 sts; work in patt across—22 (26, 30, 34) sts.

Row 2:
Work in patt across.

Row 3:
Bind off 2 sts; work in patt across—20 (24, 28, 32) sts.

Row 4:
Work in patt across.

Row 5:
K1, K2 tog; work in patt across—19 (23, 27, 31) sts.

Row 6:
Work in patt to last 3 sts; P2 tog; P1—18 (22, 26, 30) sts.

Continuing in patt, dec one st on neck edge 4 (5, 5, 5) times; AT THE SAME TIME, when piece measures same as back to shoulder shaping, on wrong side rows, bind off 5 (6, 8, 9) sts twice, then bind off rem 6 (7, 7, 9) sts.

Sleeve (make 2)

Cast on 30 (30, 30, 34) sts.

For Size Small Only:

Row 1 *(right side)*:
K2; * P2, K2; rep from * across.

Row 2:
P2; * K2, P2; rep from * across.

Row 3:
Rep Row 2.

Rows 4 and 5:
Rep Row 1.

Row 6:
Inc (knit in front and back of next st); P1; * K2, P2; rep from * 5 times more; K2, P1, inc—32 sts.

Row 7:
K1, P2; * K2, P2; rep from * 6 times more; K1.

Rows 8 and 9:
P1, K2; * P2, K2; rep from * 6 times more; P1.

Row 10:
K1, P2; * K2, P2; rep from * 6 times more; K1.

Row 11:
Rep Row 10.

Row 12:
Inc; K2; * P2, K2; rep from * 6 times more; inc—34 sts.

Continue in patt as established, inc one st at each end of every 6th row 10 times more, then inc one st at each end of every 8th row twice. At end of last inc row—58 sts.

Work even in patt (without inc) until sleeve measures 19³/₄" from cast-on edge.

Bind off.

For Sizes Medium, Large, and X-Large Only:

Row 1 (right side):
K2; * P2, K2; rep from * across.

Row 2:
P2; * K2, P2; rep from * across.

Row 3:
Rep Row 2.

Row 4:
Inc (knit in front and back of next st); K1; * P2, K2; rep from * 5 (5, 6) more; P2, K1, inc—32 (32, 36) sts.

Row 5:
P1, K2; * P2, K2; rep from * 6 (6, 7) times more; P1.

Row 6:
K1, P2; * K2, P2; rep from * 6 (6, 7) times more; K1.

Row 7:
Rep Row 6.

Row 8:
Inc; * K2, P2; rep from * 6 (6, 7) times more; K2, inc—34 (34, 38) sts.

Continue in patt as established, inc one st at each end of every 4th row 4 (6, 8) times more, then inc one st at each end of every 6th row 10 (8, 6) times. At end of last inc row—62 (62, 66) sts.

Work even in patt (without inc) until sleeve measures 19" (18¹/₄", 17¹/₂") from cast-on edge.

Bind off.

Sew shoulder seams.

Edging
With right side facing you and lower edge of back at top, with crochet hook, join yarn in right side seam; ch 1, sc in same sp; sc in each cast-on st to next corner; 3 sc in corner; working along right front edge, sc in side of each row to next corner; 3 sc in corner; working along neck edge, sc in each bound-off st, in side of each row, in each st across back, in side of each row, and in each bound-off st to next corner; 3 sc in corner; working along left front edge, sc in side of each row to next corner; 3 sc in corner; working along lower edge, sc in each cast-on st to first sc; join in first sc.

Finish off and weave in ends.

Finishing
Step 1:
Referring to diagram, sew sleeves to body.

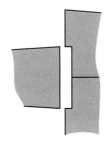

Step 2:
Sew sleeve and side seams.
Step 3:
Sew button opposite buttonhole.

Dainty Cardigan

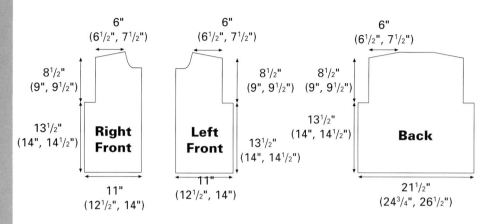

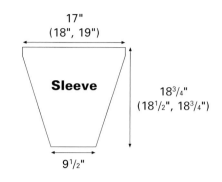

All measurements are approximate.

Sizes:
Medium   Large   X-Large

Body Chest Measurement:
36"   40"   44"

Garment Chest Measurement:
$44^{1}/_{2}$" $50^{3}/_{4}$" $56^{3}/_{4}$"

Note: *Instructions are written for size medium; changes for larger sizes are in parentheses. If only one number is given, it is the same for all sizes.*

Materials:
Lion Brand Microspun, Lily White #100
For Size Medium: 11 skeins
For Size Large: 12 skeins
For Size X-Large: 14 skeins
Size 4 (3.5mm) knitting needles,
   or size required for gauge
Markers
Two stitch holders
Seven buttons, $^3/_4$"-diameter
Sewing needle and matching thread

Gauge:
In stockinette stitch (knit one row, purl one row):
$6^{1}/_{2}$ sts = 1"

Instructions

Back
Cast on 141 (161, 181) sts.

Border:

Rows 1 *(right side)* ***through 6:***
Knit.

Row 7:
K1; * YO, K3, sl 2 tog as to knit, K1, P2SSO; K3, YO, K1; rep from * 13 (15, 17) times more.

Row 8:
P2; * YO, P2, sl 2 tog tbl, P1, P2SSO; P2, YO, P3; rep from * 12 (14, 16) times more; YO, P2, sl 2 tog tbl, P1, P2SSO; P2, YO, P2.

Row 9:
K3; * YO, K1, sl 2 tog as to knit, K1, P2SSO; K1, YO, K5; rep from * 12 (14, 16) times more; YO, K1, sl 2 tog as to knit, K1, P2SSO; K1, YO, K3.

Row 10:
P4; * YO, sl 2 tog tbl, P1, P2SSO; YO, P7; rep from * 12 (14, 16) times more; YO, sl 2 tog tbl, P1, P2SSO; YO, P4.

Rows 11 and 12:
Knit.

Rows 13 through 24:
Rep Rows 7 through 12 twice more.

Body:

Row 1 *(right side):*
Knit.

Row 2:
K1; * P4, K1; rep from * across.

Rows 3 through 6:
Rep Rows 1 and 2 twice more.

Rows 7 and 8:
Knit.

Rep Rows 1 through 8 of body until piece measures about $13^{1}/_{2}$" (14", $14^{1}/_{2}$") from cast-on edge, ending by working a wrong side row.

Armhole Shaping:

Row 1 *(right side):*
Bind off 10 (15, 20) sts; work in patt across.

Row 2:
Rep Row 1. At end of Row 2—
121 (131, 141) sts.

Continue in patt until piece measures 22" (23", 24") from cast-on edge, ending by working a wrong side row.

Shoulder Shaping:

Row 1 *(right side):*
Bind off 10 (11, 12) sts; work in patt across.

Rows 2 through 6:
Rep Row 1. At end of Row 6—61 (65, 69) sts.

Row 7:
Bind off 9 (11, 13) sts; work in patt across.

 continued on page 30

Dainty Cardigan

Row 8:
Rep Row 7.

Bind off rem 43 sts.

Left Front
Cast on 71 **(81, 91)** sts.

Border:

Rows 1 (right side) through 6:
Knit.

Row 7:
* K1, YO, K3, sl 2 tog as to knit, K1, P2SSO; K3, YO; rep from * 6 **(7, 8)** times more; K1.

Row 8:
P2; * YO, P2, sl 2 tog tbl, P1, P2SSO; P2, YO, P3; rep from * 5 **(6, 7)** times more; YO, P2, sl 2 tog tbl, P1, P2SSO; P2, YO, P2.

Row 9:
K3; * YO, K1, sl 2 tog as to knit, K1, P2SSO; K1, YO, K5; rep from * 5 **(6, 7)** times more; YO, K1, sl 2 tog as to knit, K1, P2SSO; K1, YO, K3.

Row 10:
P4; * YO, sl 2 tog tbl, P1, P2SSO; YO, P7; rep from * 5 **(6, 7)** times more; YO, sl 2 tog tbl, P1, P2SSO; YO, P4.

Rows 11 and 12:
Knit.

Rows 13 through 24:
Rep Rows 7 through 12 twice more.

Body:

Row 1 (right side):
Knit.

Row 2:
K1; * P4, K1; rep from * across.

Rows 3 through 6:
Rep Rows 1 and 2 twice more.

Rows 7 and 8:
Knit.

Rep Rows 1 through 8 of Body until piece measures same as Back to Armhole Shaping, ending by working a wrong side row.

Armhole Shaping:

Row 1 (right side):
Bind off 10 **(15, 20)** sts; work in patt across—61 **(66, 71)** sts.

Row 2:
Work in patt across.

Continue in patt until piece measures about 20½" **(21½", 22½")** from cast-on edge, ending by working a wrong side row.

Neck and Shoulder Shaping:

Row 1 (right side):
Work in patt across.

Row 2:
Bind off 10 sts; work in patt across—51 **(56, 61)** sts.

Row 3:
Work in patt across.

Row 4:
Bind off 5 sts; work in patt across—46 **(51, 56)** sts.

Row 5:
Work in patt across.

Rows 6 and 7:
Rep Rows 4 and 5. At end of Row 7—41 **(46, 51)** sts.

Row 8:
P1, sl 1 as to purl, P1, PSSO; work in patt across.

Row 9:
Work in patt across.

Row 10:
Rep Row 8.

Row 11:
Bind off 10 **(11, 12)** sts; work in patt across.

Row 12:
Work in patt across.

Rows 13 and 14:
Rep Rows 11 and 12.

Row 15:
Rep Row 11.

Bind off rem 9 **(11, 13)** sts.

Right Front
Work same as Left Front to Armhole Shaping.

Armhole Shaping:

Row 1 (right side):
Work in patt across.

Row 2:
Bind off 10 **(15, 20)** sts; work in patt across—61 **(66, 71)** sts.

Continue in patt until piece measures about 20½", **(21½", 22½")** from cast-on

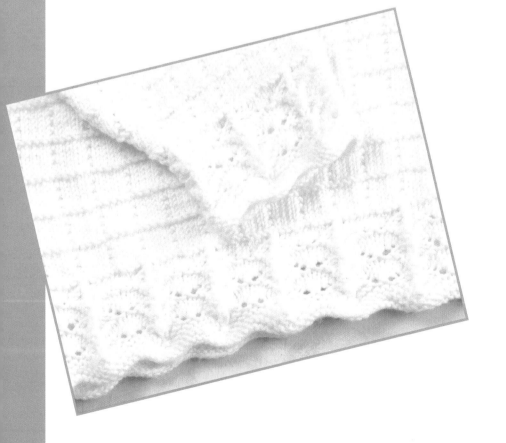

edge, ending by working a wrong side row.

Neck and Shoulder Shaping:

Row 1 *(right side):*
Bind off 10 sts; work in patt across—51 **(**56, 61**)** sts.

Row 2:
Work in patt across.

Row 3:
Bind off 5 sts; work in patt across—46 **(**51, 56**)** sts.

Row 4:
Work in patt across.

Rows 5 and 6:
Rep Rows 3 and 4. At end of Row 6—41 **(**46, 51**)** sts.

Row 7:
K1, sl 1 as to knit, K1, PSSO; work in patt across.

Row 8:
Work in patt across.

Row 9:
Rep Row 7.

Row 10:
Bind off 10 **(**11, 12**)** sts; work in patt across.

Row 11:
Work in patt across.

Rows 12 through 15:
Rep Rows 10 and 11 twice more.

Bind off rem 9 **(**11, 13**)** sts.

Sleeve **(**make 2**)**
Cast on 61 sts.

Border:

Rows 1 *(right side)* **through 6:**
Knit.

Row 7:
* K1, YO, K3, sl 2 tog as to knit, K1, P2SSO; K3, YO; rep from * 5 times more; K1.

Row 8:
P2; * YO, P2, sl 2 tog tbl, P1, P2SSO; P2, YO, P3; rep from * 4 times more; YO, P2, sl 2 tog tbl, P1, P2SSO; P2, YO, P2.

Row 9:
K3; * YO, K1, sl 2 tog as to knit, K1, P2SSO; K1, YO, K5; rep from * 4 times more; YO, K1, sl 2 tog as to knit, K1, P2SSO; K1, YO, K3.

Row 10:
P4; * YO, sl 2 tog tbl, P1, P2SSO; YO, P7; rep from * 4 times more; YO, sl 2 tog tbl, P1, P2SSO; YO, P4.

Rows 11 and 12:
Knit.

Rows 13 through 24:
Rep Rows 7 through 12 twice more.

Body:

For Size Medium Only:

Row 1 *(right side):*
Knit.

Row 2:
K1; * P4, K1; rep from * across.

Rows 3 and 4:
Rep Rows 1 and 2.

Row 5:
Inc **(**knit in front and back of next st**)**; knit to last st; inc—63 sts.

Row 6:
P1, K1; * P4, K1; rep from * to last st; P1.

Rows 7 and 8:
Knit.

Row 9:
Rep Row 5. At end of row—65 sts.

Row 10:
P2, K1; * P4, K1; rep from * to last 2 sts; P2.

Row 11:
Knit.

Row 12:
Rep Row 10.

Row 13:
Rep Row 5. At end of row—67 sts.

Row 14:
P3, K1; * P4, K1; rep from * to last 3 sts; P3.

Rows 15 and 16:
Knit.

Row 17:
Rep Row 5. At end of row—69 sts.

Row 18:
P4; * K1, P4; rep from * across.

Row 19:
Knit.

Row 20:
Rep Row 18.

Row 21:
Rep Row 5. At end of row—71 sts.

Row 22:
Rep Row 2.

Rows 23 and 24:
Knit.

Row 25:
Rep Row 5. At end of row—73 sts.

Row 26:
Rep Row 6.

Row 27:
Knit.

Row 28:
Rep Row 6.

Row 29:
Rep Row 5. At end of row—75 sts.

Row 30:
Rep Row 10.

Rows 31 and 32:
Knit.

Row 33:
Rep Row 5. At end of row—77 sts.

Row 34:
Rep Row 14.

Row 35:
Knit.

Row 36:
Rep Row 14.

Row 37:
Rep Row 5. At end of row—79 sts.

Row 38:
Rep Row 18.

Rows 39 and 40:
Knit.

Row 41:
Rep Row 5. At end of row—81 sts.

Rows 42 through 73:
Rep Rows 2 through 33. At end of Row 73—97 sts.

Continue in patt, inc one st each side every 6th row 7 times—111 sts.

Work even in patt **(**without inc**)** until sleeve measures about 18³/₄" from cast-on edge.

Bind off.

For Sizes Large, and X-Large Only:

Row 1 *(right side):*
Inc **(**knit in front and back of next st**)**; knit to last st; inc—63 sts.

Row 2:
P1, K1; * P4, K1; rep from * to last st; P1.

Row 3:
Rep Row 1. At end of row—65 sts.

Row 4:
P2; * K1, P4; rep from * to last 3 sts; K1, P2.

Row 5:
Rep Row 1. At end of row—67 sts.

Row 6:
P3; * K1, P4; rep from * to last 4 sts;

Dainty Cardigan

K1, P3.

Row 7:
Rep Row 1. At end of row—69 sts.

Row 8:
Knit.

Row 9:
Rep Row 1. At end of row—71 sts.

Row 10:
K1; ***** P4, K1; rep from ***** across.

Row 11:
Rep Row 1. At end of row—73 sts.

Row 12:
Rep Row 2.

For Size Large Only:

Row 13:
Knit.

Row 14:
P1, K1; ***** P4, K1; rep from ***** to last st; P1.

Row 15:
Rep Row 1. At end of row—75 sts.

Rows 16 and 17:
Knit.

Row 18:
Rep Row 4.

Row 19:
Rep Row 1. At end of row—77 sts.

Row 20:
Rep Row 6.

Row 21:
Knit.

Row 22:
Rep Row 6.

Row 23:
Rep Row 1. At end of row—79 sts.

Rows 24 and 25:
Knit.

Row 26:
P4; * K1, P4; rep from * across.

Row 27:
Rep Row 1. At end of row—81 sts.

Row 28:
Rep Row 10.

Row 29:
Knit.

Row 30:
Rep Row 10.

Row 31:
Rep Row 1. At end of row—83 sts.

Rows 32 and 33:
Knit.

Continue in patt, inc one st each side of every 4th row 17 times—117 sts.

Work even in patt (without inc) until sleeve measures about 18¹/₂" from cast-on edge, ending by working a right side row.

Bind off.

For Size X-Large Only:

Rows 13 through 22:
Rep Rows 3 through 12 once more. At end of Row 22—83 sts.

Rows 23 through 28:
Rep Rows 3 through 8 once. At end of Row 28—89 sts.

Continue in patt, inc one st each side every 4th row 17 times—123 sts.

Work even in patt (without inc) until sleeve measures about 18³/₄", ending by working a right side row.

Bind off.

Sew shoulder seams.

Neck Band
With right side facing you, beg at right front edge, pick up and knit 92 sts evenly spaced around neckline.

Row 1:
Knit.

Rep Row 1 until neck band measures 1".

Bind off.

Button Band
With right side of left front facing you, pick up and knit 90 (94, 98) sts evenly spaced along left front edge. Work same as for Neck Band.

Buttonhole Band
Place 7 markers evenly spaced along right front band for buttonholes. With right side of right front facing you, pick up and knit 90 (94, 98) sts evenly spaced along right front edge.

Row 1:
Knit.

Rep Row 1 until band measures ¹/₂".

Next Row:
Knit to first marker; bind off 3 sts; * knit to next marker; bind off 3 sts; rep from * 5 times more; knit rem sts.

Next Row:
Knit to first bound-off st; cast on 3 sts; * knit to next bound off; cast on 3 sts; rep from * 5 times more; knit rem sts.

Next Row:
Knit.
Rep last row until buttonhole band measures 1".

Bind off.

Finishing

Step 1:
Referring to diagram, sew sleeves to body.

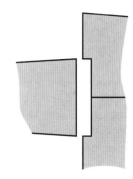

Step 2:
Sew sleeve and side seams.

Step 3:
Sew buttons opposite buttonholes.

Lace Panel Pullover

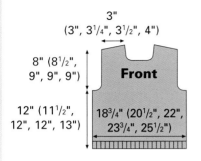

3"
(3", 3¹/₄", 3¹/₂", 4")

8" (8¹/₂",
9", 9", 9")

Front

12" (11¹/₂",
12", 12", 13")

18³/₄" (20¹/₂", 22",
23³/₄", 25¹/₂")

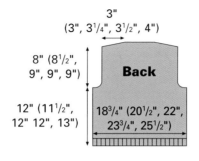

3"
(3", 3¹/₄", 3¹/₂", 4")

8" (8¹/₂",
9", 9", 9")

Back

12" (11¹/₂",
12" 12", 13")

18³/₄" (20¹/₂", 22",
23³/₄", 25¹/₂")

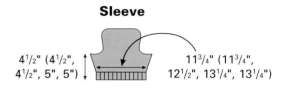

Sleeve

4¹/₂" (4¹/₂",
4¹/₂", 5", 5")

11³/₄" (11³/₄",
12¹/₂", 13¹/₄", 13¹/₄")

All measurements are approximate.

Sizes:
Small   Medium   Large   1X   2X

Body Chest Measurement:
32"   36"   38"   42"   46"

**Garment Chest
Measurement:**
37¹/₂"   41"   44"   47¹/₂"   51"
*Note: Instructions are written for
size small; changes for larger sizes
are in parentheses. If only one
number given, it is the same for
all sizes.*

Materials:
Lion Brand Microspun, Coral #103
For Size Small: 5 skeins
For Size Medium: 5 skeins
For Size Large: 6 skeins
For Size 1X: 7 skeins
For Size 2X: 8 skeins
Size 4 (3.5mm) knitting needles,
  or size required for gauge
Size 4 (3.5mm) 16" circular knitting
  needle
Markers

Gauge:
In stockinette stitch (knit one row,
purl one row):
6 sts = 1"

Special Abbreviation

Slip, Slip, Knit (SSK):
Slip next 2 sts, one at a time, as to knit
(**Fig 1**); insert left-hand needle through
both sts from left to right (**Fig 2**); K2
tog—SSK made.

Fig 1

Fig 2

Instructions

Back
Cast on 117 (127, 137, 147, 157) sts.

Ribbing:
***Row 1** (right side)*:
K1; * P1, K1; rep from * across.

***Row 2**:*
P1; * K1, P1; rep from * across.

Rep Rows 1 and 2 until ribbing measures about 2" from cast-on edge,
ending by working a wrong side row.

Body:
***Row 1** (right side)*:
K45 (50, 55, 60, 65); place marker, P1,
K2 tog; YO, K1, YO, SSK (see Special
Abbreviation); P1, K4, K2 tog; YO, K1,
YO, SSK; K4, P1, K2 tog; YO, K1, YO,
SSK; P1; place marker, K45 (50, 55,
60, 65).

*Note: Slip markers as you come
to them.*

Row 2 and all wrong-side rows:
P45 (50, 55, 60, 65); K1, P5, K1, P13, K1,
P5, K1, P45 (50, 55, 60, 65).

***Row 3**:*
K45 (50, 55, 60, 65); P1, K2 tog; YO, K1,
YO, SSK; P1, K3, K2 tog; YO, K3, YO,
SSK; K3, P1, K2 tog; YO, K1, YO, SSK;
P1, K45 (50, 55, 60, 65).

***Row 5**:*
K45 (50, 55, 60, 65); P1, K2 tog; YO, K1,
YO, SSK; P1, K2, K2 tog; YO, K5, YO,
SSK; K2, P1, K2 tog; YO, K1, YO, SSK;
P1, K45 (50, 55, 60, 65).

***Row 7**:*
K45 (50, 55, 60, 65); P1, K2 tog; YO,
K1, YO, SSK; P1, K1, K2 tog; YO, K1,
K2 tog; YO, K1, YO, SSK; K1, YO, SSK;
K1, P1, K2 tog; YO, K1, YO, SSK; P1,
K45 (50, 55, 60, 65).

***Row 9**:*
K45 (50, 55, 60, 65); P1, K2 tog; YO,
K1, YO, SSK; P1, K2 tog; YO, K1,
K2 tog; YO, K3, YO, SSK; K1, YO, SSK;
P1, K2 tog; YO, K1, YO, SSK; P1, K45
(50, 55, 60, 65).

***Row 11**:*
K45 (50, 55, 60, 65); P1, K2 tog; YO, K1,
YO, SSK; P1, K2, YO, K2 tog; K1, YO,
sl 2 as to knit, K1, P2SSO; YO, K1,
K2 tog; YO, K2, P1, K2 tog; YO, K1, YO,
SSK; P1, K45 (50, 55, 60, 65).

***Row 13**:*
K45 (50, 55, 60, 65); P1, K2 tog; YO, K1,
YO, SSK; P1, K3, YO, K2 tog; K3, SSK;
YO, K3, P1, K2 tog; YO, K1, YO, SSK;
P1, K45 (50, 55, 60, 65).

***Row 15**:*
K45 (50, 55, 60, 65); P1, K2 tog; YO, K1,
YO, SSK; P1, K4, YO, SSK; K1,
K2 tog; YO, K4, P1, K2 tog; YO, K1, YO,
SSK; P1, K45 (50, 55, 60, 65).

continued on page 36

Lace Panel Pullover

Row 17:
K45 (50, 55, 60, 65); P1, K2 tog; YO, K1, YO, SSK; P1, K5, YO, sl 2 as to knit, K1, P2SSO; YO, K5, P1, K2 tog; YO, K1, YO, SSK; P1, K45 (50, 55, 60, 65).

Row 18:
Rep Row 2.

Rep Rows 1 through 18 of body until piece measures about 12" (11½", 12", 12", 13") from cast-on edge, ending by working a wrong side row.

Armhole Shaping:

Row 1 (*right side*):
Bind off 6 sts; work in patt across.

Row 2:
Rep Row 1. At end of row—105 (115, 125, 135, 145) sts.

Row 3:
Bind off 4 sts; work in patt across.

Row 4:
Rep Row 3. At end of row—97 (107, 117, 127, 137) sts.

Row 5:
Bind off 2 (2, 2, 3, 3) sts; work in patt across.

Rows 6 through 8 (10, 10, 12, 14):
Rep Row 5. At end of last row—89 (95, 105, 103, 107) sts.

For Sizes Small, and Medium Only:

Row 9:
K1, K2 tog; work in patt to last 3 sts; SSK; K1—87 (93) sts.

Row 10:
Work in patt across.

Rows 11 through 16 (18):
Rep Rows 9 and 10 three (4) times more. At end of Row 16 (18)—81 (85) sts.

Work even in patt (without dec) until piece measures about 20" (20") from cast-on edge, ending by working a wrong side row.

Continue with Shoulder Shaping.

For Size Large Only:

Row 11:
K1, K2 tog; work in patt to last 3 sts; SSK; K1—103 sts.

Row 12:
P1, P2 tog tbl; work in patt to last 3 sts; P2 tog; P1—101 sts.

Row 13:
K1, K2 tog; work in patt to last 3 sts; SSK; K1—99 sts.

Row 14:
Work in patt across.

Rows 15 through 26:
Rep Rows 13 and 14 six times more. At end of Row 26—87 sts.

Work even in patt (without dec) until piece measures about 21" from cast-on edge, ending by working a wrong side row.

Continue with Shoulder Shaping.

For Size 1X Only:

Row 13:
K1, K2 tog; work in patt to last 3 sts; SSK; K1—101 sts.

Row 14:
P1, P2 tog tbl; work in patt to last 3 sts; P2 tog; P1—99 sts.

Rows 15 and 16:
Rep Rows 13 and 14. At end of Row 16—95 sts.

Row 17:
Work in patt across.

Row 18:
K1, K2 tog; work in patt to last 3 sts; SSK; K1—93 sts.

Rows 19 and 20:
Rep Rows 17 and 18. At end of Row 20—91 sts.

Work even in patt (without dec) until piece measures about 21" from cast-on edge, ending by working a wrong side row.

Continue with Shoulder Shaping.

For Size 2X Only:

Row 15:
K1, K2 tog; work in patt to last 3 sts; SSK; K1—105 sts.

Row 16:
P1, P2 tog tbl; work in patt to last 3 sts; P2 tog; P1—103 sts.

Rows 17 through 20:
Rep Rows 15 and 16 twice more. At end of Row 20—95 sts.

Row 21:
Work in patt across.

Row 22:
Rep Row 16. At end of row—93 sts. Work even in patt (without dec) until piece measures about 22" from cast-on edge, ending by working a wrong side row.
Continue with Shoulder Shaping.

Shoulder Shaping:

Row 1 (*right side*):
Bind off 4 (5, 5, 5, 6) sts; work in patt across.

Rows 2 through 6:
Rep Row 1.

Row 7:
Bind off 5 (4, 5, 7, 5) sts; work in patt across.

Row 8:
Rep Row 7.

Bind off rem 47 sts.

Front
Work same as for Back until piece has 24 rows less than back, ending by working a wrong side row.

Neck Shaping:

Row 1 (*right side*):
For left shoulder, work in patt across first 31 (33, 34, 36, 37) sts; join second skein of yarn; bind off next 19 sts; for right shoulder, work in patt across rem sts.
Note: *Work across both shoulders at same time with separate skeins of yarn.*

Row 2:
Work in patt across.

Row 3:
On left shoulder, work in patt across; on right shoulder, bind off next 4 sts; work in patt across.

Row 4:
On right shoulder, work in patt across; on left shoulder, bind off 4 sts; work in patt across—27 (29, 30, 32, 33) sts on each shoulder.

Row 5:
On left shoulder, work in patt across; on right shoulder, bind off 2 sts; work in patt across.

Row 6:
On right shoulder, work in patt across; on left shoulder, bind off 2 sts; work in patt across—25 (27, 28, 30, 31) sts on each shoulder.

Rows 7 and 8:
Rep Rows 5 and 6. At end of Row 8—23 (25, 26, 28, 29) sts on each shoulder.

Row 9:
On left shoulder, work in patt to last 3 sts; SSK; K1; on right shoulder, K1, K2 tog; work in patt across rem sts—22 (24, 25, 27, 28) sts on each shoulder.

Row 10:
On right shoulder, work in patt to last 3 sts; P2 tog; P1; on left shoulder, P1, P2 tog tbl; work in patt across rem

American School of Needlework • San Marcos, CA 92069 • ASNpub.com sts—21 (23, 24, 26, 27) sts on each shoulder.

Rows 11 and 12:
Rep Rows 9 and 10. At end of Row 12—19 (21, 22, 24, 25) sts.

Row 13:
Rep Row 9.

Row 14:
Work in patt across both shoulders.

Rows 15 and 16:
Rep Rows 13 and 14. At end of Row 16—17 (19, 20, 22, 23) sts on each shoulder.

Shoulder Shaping (all sizes):

Row 1:
Bind off 4 (5, 5, 5, 6) sts; work in patt across both shoulders.

Row 2:
Bind off 4 (5, 5, 5, 6) sts; work in patt across both shoulders.

Rows 3 through 6:
Rep Rows 1 and 2 twice more. At end of Row 6—5 (4, 5, 7, 5) sts on each shoulder.

Row 7:
Bind off 5 (4, 5, 7, 5) sts; work in patt across right shoulder.

Bind off rem sts.

Sleeve (make 2)

Ribbing:
Cast on 70 (70, 74, 80, 80) sts.

Row 1 (right side):
* K1, P1; rep from * across.

Rep Row 1 until piece measures 2" from cast-on edge.

Body:

Row 1 (right side):
Knit.

Row 2:
Purl.

Row 3:
Inc (knit in front and back of next st); knit to last st; inc—72 (72, 76, 82, 82) sts.

Row 4:
Purl.

For Sizes Small, 1X, and 2X Only:

Rows 5 through 16 (20, 20):
Rep Rows 1 through 4 three (4, 4) times more. At end of last row—78 (90, 90) sts.

Continue with For All Sizes below.

For Size Medium Only:

Rows 5 through 14:
Rep Rows 3 and 4 five times more.

At end of Row 14—82 sts.

Rows 15 through 18:
Rep Rows 1 through 4 once. At end of Row 18—84 sts.

Continue with For All Sizes below.

For Size Large Only:

Rows 5 and 6:
Rep Rows 3 and 4. At end of Row 6—78 sts.

Rows 7 through 18:
Rep Rows 1 through 4 three times. At end of Row 18—84 sts.

Continue with For All Sizes.

For All Sizes:

Work in stockinette st (knit one row, purl one row) until piece measures 4¹/₂" (4¹/₂", 4¹/₂", 5", 5") from cast-on edge, ending by working a wrong side row.

Cap Shaping:

Row 1 (right side):
Bind off 6 sts; knit across.

Row 2:
Bind off 6 sts; purl across—66 (72, 72, 78, 78) sts.

Row 3:
K1, K2 tog; knit to last 3 sts; SSK; K1—64 (70, 70, 76, 76) sts.

Row 4:
Purl.

Row 5:
Knit.

Row 6:
Purl.

For Size Small Only:

Rows 7 through 18:
Rep Rows 3 through 6 three times more. At end of Row 18—58 sts.

Rows 15 through 44:
Rep Rows 3 and 4 fifteen times. At end of Row 44—28 sts.

Row 45:
Bind off 2 sts; knit across.

Row 46:
Bind off 2 sts; purl across.

Rows 47 and 48:
Rep Rows 45 and 46. At end of Row 48—20 sts.

Bind off.

For Size Medium Only:

Rows 7 through 48:
Rep Rows 3 and 4 twenty-one times. At end of Row 48—28 sts.

Row 49:
Bind off 2 sts; knit across.

Row 50:
Bind off 2 sts; purl across.

Rows 51 and 52:
Rep Rows 49 and 50. At end of Row 52—20 sts.

Bind off.

For Sizes Large, 1X, and 2X Only:

Rows 7 through 10:
Rep Rows 3 through 6 once more. At end of Row 10—68 (74, 74) sts.

Rows 11 through 52 (48, 48):
Rep Rows 3 and 4 twenty-one (19, 19) times. At end of last row—26 (28, 28) sts.

Row 53 (49, 49):
Bind off 2 sts; knit across.

Row 54 (50, 50):
Bind off 2 sts; purl across.

Rows 55 (51, 51) and 56 (52, 52):
Rep Rows 53 (49, 49) and 54 (50, 50). At end of last row—26 (28, 28) sts.

Bind off.

Sew shoulder seams.

Neck Band
Hold sweater with right side facing you and right shoulder at top; with circular needle, pick up and knit 118 sts including sts around neckline.

Rnds 1 through 8:
Knit.

Bind off loosely allowing neckband to roll.

Finishing
Step 1:
Referring to diagram, sew sleeves to body.

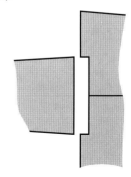

Step 2:
Sew sleeve and side seams.

Oversized Chevron Cardigan

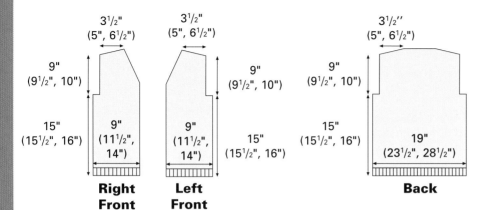

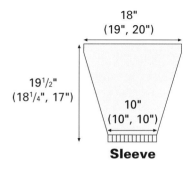

All measurements are approximate.

Sizes:

Small	Medium	Large

Body Chest Measurement:

32"	36"	40"

Garment Chest Measurement:

37"	46½"	56½"

Note: *Instructions are written for size small; changes for larger sizes are in parentheses.*

Materials:

Lion Brand Wool-Ease Thick and Quick, Fisherman #099
For Size Small: 9 skeins
For Size Medium: 10 skeins
For Size Large: 11 skeins
Size 13 (9mm) 29" circular knitting needle, or size required for gauge
3 stitch holders
Seven decorative buttons
Note: *Buttons by JHB International, Autumn Bounty #80658*
Sewing needle and matching thread

Gauge:

In pattern stitch:
10 sts = 4"
16 rows = 4"

Instructions

Back

Ribbing:
Cast on 47 (59, 71) sts.

Row 1 *(wrong side):*
K1; * P1, K1; rep from * across.

Row 2 *(right side):*
P1; * K1, P1; rep from * across.

Rows 3 and 4:
Rep Rows 1 and 2.

Row 5:
Rep Row 1.

Body:

Row 1 *(right side):*
K5; * P1, K5; rep from * across.

Row 2:
K1, P3, K1; * K2, P3, K1; rep from * across.

Row 3:
P2; * K1, P2; rep from * across.

Row 4:
P1, K3; * P3, K3; rep from * to last st; P1.

Row 5:
K2, P1; * K5, P1; rep from * to last 2 sts; K2.

Row 6:
Purl.

Rep Rows 1 through 6 until piece measures about 15" (15½", 16") from cast-on edge, ending by working a wrong side row.

Armhole Shaping:

Row 1 *(right side):*
Bind off 3 (4, 5) sts; work in patt across—44 (55, 66) sts.

Row 2:
Rep Row 1—41 (51, 61) sts.

Work even in patt (without dec) until piece measures about 24" (25", 26") from cast-on edge, ending by working a wrong side row.

Shoulder Shaping:

Row 1 *(right side):*
Bind off 6 (8, 11) sts; work in patt across—35 (43, 50) sts.

Row 2:
Rep Row 1—29 (35, 39) sts.

Row 3:
Bind off 6 (9, 11) sts; work in patt across—23 (26, 28) sts.

Row 4:
Rep Row 3—17 (17, 17) sts.

Bind off rem sts.

Pocket Lining (make 2):
Cast on 15 sts.

Row 1 *(right side):*
Knit.

Row 2:
Purl.

Rep Rows 1 and 2 until piece measures about 5", ending by working a wrong side row.

Slip sts onto stitch holder.

Left Front

Cast on 23 (29, 35) sts.

Work same as Back until piece measures about 6½" from cast-on edge, ending by working a wrong side row.

Place Pocket Linings:

Row 1 *(right side):*
Work in patt across first 4 (7, 10) sts; slip next 15 sts onto stitch holder; slip pocket lining sts from stitch holder onto left-hand needle; work in patt across

continued on page 40

Oversized Chevron Cardigan

15 pocket lining sts and next 4 (7, 10) sts.

Continue in patt until piece measures same as back to armhole shaping.

Armhole Shaping:

Row 1 *(right side)*:
Bind off 3 (4, 5) sts; work in patt across—20 (25, 30) sts.

Row 2:
Work in patt across.

Continue in patt until piece measures about 16" (17", 18") from beg, ending by working a wrong side row.

Neck Shaping:

Row 1 *(right side)*:
Work in patt across.

Row 2:
P2 tog; work in patt across—19 (24, 29) sts.

Rows 3 through 5:
Rep Row 1.

Rows 6 through 29:
Rep Rows 2 through 5 six times more. At end of Row 29—13 (18, 23) sts.

Row 30:
Rep Row 2—12 (17, 22) sts.

Work even (without dec) in patt until piece measures same as back to Row 2 of Shoulder Shaping.

Shoulder Shaping:

Row 1 *(right side)*:
Bind off 6 (8, 11) sts; work in patt across—6 (9, 11) sts.

Bind off rem sts.

Right Front

Work same as Left Front to Armhole Shaping.

Armhole Shaping:

Row 1 *(right side)*:
Work in patt across.

Row 2:
Bind off 3 (4, 5) sts; work in patt across—20 (25, 30) sts.

Work even in patt until piece measures same as Left Front to Neck Shaping, ending by working a wrong side row.

Neck Shaping:

Row 1 *(right side)*:
K2 tog; work in patt across—19 (24, 29) sts.

Row 2:
Work in patt across.

Rows 3 and 4:
Rep Row 2.

Rows 5 through 28:
Rep Rows 1 through 4 six times more. At end of Row 28—13 (18, 23) sts.

Rows 29 and 30:
Rep Rows 1 and 2. At end of Row 30—12 (17, 22) sts.

Work even (without dec) until piece measures same as back to Shoulder Shaping, ending by working a right side row.

Shoulder Shaping:

Row 1 *(wrong side)*:
Bind off 6 (8, 11) sts; work in patt across—6 (9, 11) sts.

Bind off rem sts.

Left Pocket Edge:

Hold left front with right side facing you, slip 15 pocket sts from stitch holder to left-hand needle.

Row 1 *(right side)*:
K1; * P1, K1; rep from * across.

Row 2:
P1; * K1, P1; rep from * across.

Rows 3 and 4:
Rep Rows 1 and 2.

Bind off loosely.

Right Pocket Edge:

Holding right front with right side facing you, work same as left pocket edge.

Sleeve (make 2)
Cast on 27 sts.

Ribbing:

Row 1 *(wrong side)*:
K1; * P1, K1; rep from * across.

Row 2 *(right side)*:
P1; * K1, P1; rep from * across.

Rows 3 and 4:
Rep Rows 1 and 2.

Row 5:
Inc (knit in front and back of next st); P1; * K1, P1; rep from * to last st; inc—29 sts.

Body:

For Size Small Only:

Row 1 *(right side)*:
K5; * P1, K5; rep from * across.

Row 2:
K1, P3; * K3, P3; rep from * 3 times more; K1.

Row 3:
P2; * K1, P2; rep from * across.

Row 4:
P1, K3; * P3, K3; rep from * 3 times more; P1.

Row 5:
K2, P1; * K5, P1; rep from * 3 times more; K2.

Row 6:
Purl.

Row 7:
Rep Row 1.

Row 8:
Inc; P3; * K3, P3; rep from * 3 times more; inc—31 sts.

Row 9:
* K1, P2; rep from * 9 times more; K1.

Row 10:
P2, K3; * P3, K3; rep from * 3 times more; P2.

Row 11:
K3, P1; * K5, P1; rep from * 3 times more; K3.

Row 12:
Purl.

Row 13:
P1; * K5, P1; rep from * across.

Row 14:
K2, P3; * K3, P3; rep from * 3 times more; K2.

Row 15:
K1; * P2, K1; rep from * 9 times more.

Row 16:
Inc; P1, K3; * P3, K3; rep from * 3 times more; P1, inc—33 sts.

Rows 17 through 64:
Continue in patt, inc one st each side of every 8th row 6 times. At end of Row 64—45 sts.

Work even (without inc) until sleeve measures 19$\frac{1}{2}$" from cast-on edge, ending by working a wrong side row.

Bind off loosely.

For Sizes Medium and Large Only:

Row 1 (right side):
K5; * P1, K5; rep from * across.

Row 2:
K1, P3; * K3, P3; rep from * 3 times more; K1.

Row 3:
P2; * K1, P2; rep from * across.

Row 4:
Inc; K3; * P3, K3; rep from * 3 times more; inc—31 sts.

Row 5:
K3, P1; * K5, P1; rep from * 3 times more; K3.

Row 6:
Purl.

Rows 7:
P1; * K5, P1; rep from * 4 times more.

Row 8:
Inc; K1, P3; * K3, P3; rep from * 3 times more; K1, inc—33 sts.

Row 9:
P1; * K1, P2; rep from * 9 times more; K1, P1.

Row 10:
P3; * K3, P3; rep from * 4 times more.

Row 11:
K4, P1; * K5, P1; rep from * 3 times more; K4.

For Size Medium Only:

Row 12:
Purl.

Row 13:
K1, P1; * K5, P1; rep from * 4 times more; K1.

Row 14:
Inc; K2, P3; * K3, P3; rep from * 3 times more; K2, inc—35 sts.

Row 15:
P2; * K1, P2; rep from * 10 times more.

Row 16:
K1, P3; * K3, P3; rep from * 4 times more; K1.

Row 17:
Rep Row 1.

Row 18:
Purl.

Row 19:
K2, P1; * K5, P1; rep from * 4 times more; K2.

Row 20:
Inc; K3; * P3, K3; rep from * 4 times more; inc—37 sts.

Row 21:
* K1, P2; rep from * 11 times more; K1.

Row 22:
K2, P3; * K3, P3; rep from * 4 times more; K2.

Row 23:
P1; * K5, P1; rep from * 5 times more.

Row 24:
Purl.

Continue in patt, inc one st each side of every 6th row six times. At end of last row—49 sts.

Work even (without inc) until sleeve measures about 18$\frac{1}{4}$" from cast-on edge, ending by working a wrong side row.

Bind off loosely.

For Size Large Only:

Row 12:
Inc; purl to last st; inc—35 sts.

Row 13:
K2, P1; * K5, P1; rep from * 4 times more; K2.

Row 14:
P1, K3; * P3, K3; rep from * 4 times more; P1.

Row 15:
P2; * K1, P2; rep from * across.

Row 16:
Inc; P3; * K3, P3; rep from * 4 times more; inc—37 sts.

Rows 17:
P1; * K5, P1; rep from * across.

Row 18:
Purl.

Row 19:
K3, P1; * K5, P1; rep from * 4 times more; K3.

Row 20:
Inc; P1, K3; * P3, K3; rep from * 4 times more; P1, inc—39 sts.

Row 21:
P1, K1; * P2, K1; rep from * 11 times more; P1.

Row 22:
P3; * K3, P3; rep from * 5 times more.

Row 23:
K1, P1; * K5, P1; rep from * 5 times more; K1.

Row 24:
Inc; purl to last st; inc—41 sts.

Continue in patt, inc one st each side of every 4th row twice more, then every 6th row three times. At end of last row—51 sts.

Work even (without inc) until sleeve measures about 17" from cast-on edge, ending by working a wrong side row.

Bind off loosely.

Sew shoulder seams.

Front and Neckline Ribbing:
With right side facing you, beg at lower edge of right front, pick up and knit 157 (163, 169) sts evenly spaced along right front edge, around back of neck, and along left front edge.

Row 1 (wrong side):
P1; * K1, P1; rep from * across.

Row 2 (right side):
K1; * P1, K1; rep from * across.

On right front, place markers for seven buttonholes beg $\frac{1}{2}$" above lower edge and spacing them 2" apart.

Row 3:
P1, K1, bind off 2 sts; * work in ribbing to next marker; bind off 2 sts; rep from * 5 times more; work rem sts in ribbing.

Row 4:
Work in ribbing to first bind off; cast on 2 sts; * work in ribbing to next bind off; cast on 2 sts; rep from * 5 times more; work rem sts in ribbing.

Row 5:
Rep Row 1.

Bind off loosely in ribbing.

Finishing

Step 1:
Sew sleeves to body matching center of bound off edge of sleeve to shoulder seam.

Step 2:
Sew sleeve and side seams.

Step 3:
Sew buttons opposite buttonholes.

Textured Cabled Pullover

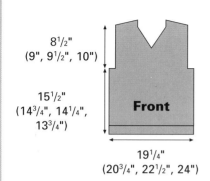

8¹/₂"
(9", 9¹/₂", 10")

15¹/₂"
(14³/₄", 14¹/₄", 13³/₄")

Front

19¹/₄"
(20³/₄", 22¹/₂", 24")

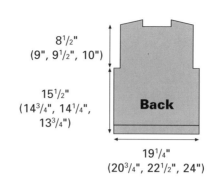

8¹/₂"
(9", 9¹/₂", 10")

15¹/₂"
(14³/₄", 14¹/₄", 13³/₄")

Back

19¹/₄"
(20³/₄", 22¹/₂", 24")

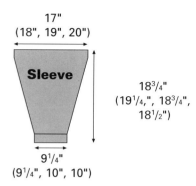

17"
(18", 19", 20")

Sleeve

18³/₄"
(19¹/₄,", 18³/₄", 18¹/₂")

9¹/₄"
(9¹/₄", 10", 10")

All measurements are approximate.

Sizes:
Small   Medium   Large   X-Large

Body Chest Measurement:
34"   36"   40"   44"

Garment Chest Measurement:
38¹/₂"   41¹/₂"   45"   48"

Note: Instructions are written for size small; changes for larger sizes are in parentheses.

Materials:
Lion Brand Al-pa-ka, Oxford Grey # 152
For Size Small: 13 skeins
For Size Medium: 13 skeins
For Size Large: 14 skeins
For Size X-Large: 14 skeins
Size 7 (4.5mm) knitting needles, or size required for gauge
Two cable needles
Two small stitch holders
Stitch markers

Gauge:
In stockinette stitch (knit one row, purl one row):
5 sts = 1"

Pattern Stitches

Cable Front (CF):
Slip next 2 sts onto cable needle and hold in front of work, K2, K2 from cable needle—CF made.

Cable Back (CB):
Slip next 2 sts onto cable needle and hold in back of work, K2, K2 from cable needle—CB made.

Cable Four Front (C4F):
Slip next 4 sts onto cable needle and hold in front of work, K4, K4 from cable needle—C4F made.

Cable Four Back (C4B):
Slip next 4 sts onto cable needle and hold in back of work, K4, K4 from cable needle—C4B made.

Cable Twist Back (CTB):
Slip next st onto cable needle and hold in back of work, K4, P1 from cable needle—CTB made.

Cable Twist Front (CTF):
Slip next 4 sts onto cable needle and hold in front of work, P1, K4 from cable needle—CTF made.

Cable Cross Back (CCB):
Slip next 4 sts onto first cable needle and hold in back of work, slip next 2 sts onto 2nd cable needle and hold in back of work, K4, P2 from 2nd cable needle, K4 from first cable needle—CCB made.

Cable Cross Front (CCF):
Slip next 4 sts onto first cable needle and hold in front of work, slip next 2 sts onto 2nd cable needle and hold in back of work, K4, P2 from 2nd cable needle, K4 from first cable needle—CCF made.

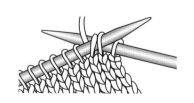

Special Abbreviation

Slip, Slip, Knit (SSK):
Slip next 2 sts, one at a time, as to knit (**Fig 1**); insert left-hand needle through both sts from left to right (**Fig 2**); K2 tog—SSK made.

Fig 1

Fig 2

Instructions

Back
Cast on 112 (120, 128, 136) sts.

Row 1 *(right side):*
* K1, P1; rep from * across.

Rep Row 1 until ribbing measures 1¹/₂" from cast-on edge, ending by working a wrong side row.

Body:
Row 1 *(right side):*
(K1, P1) 19 (21, 23, 25) times; place marker; P2, (K4, P2) twice; K8, P2, (K4, P2) twice; place marker; (K1, P1) 19 (21, 23, 25) times.
Note: *Move markers as you come to them.*

Row 2:
(K1, P1) 19 (21, 23, 25) times; (K2, P4)

continued on page 44

Textured Cabled Pullover

twice; K2, P8, K2, (P4, K2) twice; (K1, P1) 19 (21, 23, 25) times.

Row 3:
(P1, K1) 19 (21, 23, 25) times; P2, K4, P2, CF (see Pattern Stitches on page 42); P2, K8, P2, CB (see Pattern Stitches on page 42); P2, K4, P2, (P1, K1) 19 (21, 23, 25) times.

Row 4 :
(P1, K1) 19 (21, 23, 25) times; (K2, P4) twice; K2, P8, K2, (P4, K2) twice; (P1, K1) 19 (21, 23, 25) times.

Row 5:
(K1, P1) 19 (21, 23, 25) times; (P2, K4) twice; P2, C4F (see Pattern Stitches on page 42); P2, (K4, P2) twice; (K1, P1) 19 (21, 23, 25) times.

Row 6:
(K1, P1) 19 (21, 23, 25) times; (K2, P4) twice; K2, P8, K2, (P4, K2) twice; (K1, P1) 19 (21, 23, 25) times.

Row 7:
(P1, K1) 19 (21, 23, 25) times; P2, K4, P2, CF; P1, CTB (see Pattern Stitches on page 42); CTF (see Pattern Stitches on page 42); P1, CB; P2, K4, P2, (P1, K1) 19 (21, 23, 25) times.

Row 8:
(P1, K1) 19 (21, 23, 25) times; (K2, P4) twice; K1, P4, K2, P4, K1, (P4, K2) twice; (P1, K1) 19 (21, 23, 25) times.

Row 9:
(K1, P1) 19 (21, 23, 25) times; (P2, K4) twice; CTB; P2, CTF; (K4, P2) twice; (K1, P1) 19 (21, 23, 25) times.

Row 10:
(K1, P1) 19 (21, 23, 25) times; K2, P4, K2, P8, K4, P8, K2, P4, K2, (K1, P1) 19 (21, 23, 25) times.

Row 11:
(P1, K1) 19 (21, 23, 25) times; P2, K4, P2, C4B; P4, C4F; P2, K4, P2, (P1, K1) 19 (21, 23, 25) times.

Row 12:
(P1, K1) 19 (21, 23, 25) times; K2, P4, K2, P8, K4, P8, K2, P4, K2, (P1, K1) 19 (21, 23, 25) times.

Row 13:
(K1, P1) 19 (21, 23, 25) times; P2, K4, P2, K8, P4, K8, P2, K4, P2, (K1, P1) 19 (21, 23, 25) times.

Row 14:
Rep Row 10.

Row 15:
(P1, K1) 19 (21, 23, 25) times; P2, CCB (see Pattern Stitches on page 42); K4, P4, K4, CCF (see Patten Stitches on page 42); P2, (P1, K1) 19 (21, 23, 25) times.

Rows 16 through 18:
Rep Rows 12 through 14.

Row 19:
(P1, K1) 19 (21, 23, 25) times; P2, K4, P2, CF; K4, P4, K4, CB; P2, K4, P2, (P1, K1) 19 (21, 23, 25) times.

Row 20:
Rep Row 12.

Row 21:
(K1, P1) 19 (21, 23, 25) times; (P2, K4) twice; CTF; P2, CTB; (K4, P2) twice; (K1, P1) 19 (21, 23, 25) times.

Row 22:
(K1, P1) 19 (21, 23, 25) times; (K2, P4) twice; K1, P4, K2, P4, K1, (P4, K2) twice; (K1, P1) 19 (21, 23, 25) times.

Row 23:
(P1, K1) 19 (21, 23, 25) times; P2, K4, P2, CF; P1, CTF; CTB; P1, CB; P2, K4, P2, (P1, K1) 19 (21, 23, 25) times.

Rows 24 and 25:
Rep Rows 4 and 5.

Rows 26 through 28:
Rep Rows 2 through 4.

Rep Rows 1 through 28 twice more.

Armhole Shaping:

Row 1 (right side):
Bind off 6 sts; work in patt across.

Row 2:
Rep Row 1—100 (108, 116, 124) sts.

Continue in patt until piece measures about 22³/₄" from cast-on edge, ending by working a Row 28.

Neck and Shoulder Shaping:

Row 1 (right side):
For right shoulder, bind off 6 (7, 8, 9) sts; work in patt across next 20 (23, 26, 29) sts; join 2nd skein of yarn; for neck, bind off next 48 sts; for left shoulder, work in patt across.

Note: *Work both shoulders at same time with separate skeins of yarn.*

Row 2:
On left shoulder, bind off 6 (7, 8, 9) sts; work in patt across; on right shoulder, work in patt across—20 (23, 26, 29) sts on each shoulder.

Row 3:
On right shoulder, bind off 6 (7, 8, 9) sts; work in patt across; on left shoulder, work in patt across.

Row 4:
On left shoulder, bind off 6 (7, 8, 9) sts; work in patt across; on right shoulder, work in patt across—14 (16, 18, 20) sts on each shoulder.

Row 5:
On right shoulder, bind off 7 (8, 9, 10) sts; work in patt across; on left shoulder, work in patt across.

Row 6:
On left shoulder, bind off 7 (8, 9, 10) sts; work in patt across; on right shoulder, work in patt across—7 (8, 9, 10) sts on each shoulder.

Row 7:
Rep Row 5.

Bind off rem sts.

Front
Work same as Back to Armhole Shaping.

Armhole Shaping:
Work same as Armhole Shaping of Back until piece measures about about 17" from cast-on edge and you have completed a Row 24 of pattern repeat.

Neck and Shoulder Shaping:

Row 1 (right side):
For left shoulder, work in patt across first 46 (50, 54, 58) sts; sl next 4 sts onto cable needle and hold in front of work, K4, on right-hand needle, cast on 4 sts; drop yarn; for right shoulder, with 2nd skein of yarn, cast on 4 sts; K4 from cable needle; work in patt across rem sts—54 (58, 62, 66) sts on each shoulder.

Row 2:
On right shoulder, work in patt to last 8 sts; P8; on left shoulder, P8, work in patt across.

Row 3:
On left shoulder, work in patt to last 9 sts; K2 tog; K7; on right shoulder, K7, SSK (see Special Abbreviation on page 42); work in patt across—53 (57, 61, 65) sts on each shoulder.

Row 4:
On right shoulder, work in patt to last 9 sts; P2 tog tbl; P7; on left shoulder, P7, P2 tog; work in patt across—52 (56, 60, 64) sts.

Rows 5 through 10:
Rep Rows 3 and 4 three times more. At end of Row 10—46 (50, 54, 58) sts on each shoulder.

Row 11:
Rep Row 3—45 (49, 53, 57) sts on each shoulder.

Row 12:
Work even in patt (without dec) across both shoulders.

Rows 13 through 42:
Rep Rows 11 and 12 fifteen times more. At end of Row 42—30 (34, 38, 42) sts on each shoulder.

Row 43:
On left shoulder, bind off 6 (7, 8, 9) sts; work in patt to last 8 sts; K8; on right shoulder, K8, work in patt across.

Row 44:
On right shoulder, bind off 6 (7, 8, 9) sts; work in patt to last 8 sts; P8; on left shoulder, P8, work in patt across—24 (27, 30, 33) sts.

Rows 45 and 46:
Rep Rows 43 and 44. At end of Row 46—18 (20, 22, 24) sts on each shoulder.

Row 47:
On left shoulder, bind off 5 (6, 7, 8) sts; work in patt to last 8 sts; K8; on right shoulder, K8, work in patt across.

Row 48:
On right shoulder, bind off 5 (6, 7, 8) sts; work in patt to last 8 sts; P8; on left shoulder, P8, work in patt across—13 (14, 15, 16) sts on each shoulder.

Rows 49 and 50:
Rep Rows 47 and 48. At end of Row 50—8 sts on each shoulder.

Back Neck Band:

Row 1:
Knit.

Row 2:
Purl.

Rep Rows 1 and 2 until neck band will fit around back neckline when slighty stretched, meeting at center back.

Slip sts onto stitch holders.

Sleeve (make 2)
Cast on 46 (46, 50, 50) sts.

Ribbing:

Row 1 (right side):
* K1, P1; rep from * across.

Rep Row 1 until ribbing measures 1¹⁄₂" from cast-on edge.

Body:

Row 1:
* K1, P1; rep from * across.

Row 2:
Rep Row 1.

Row 3:
* P1, K1; rep from * across.

Row 4:
Rep Row 3.

Row 5:
Inc (knit in front and back of next st); * P1, K1; rep from * to last st; inc—48 (48, 52, 52) sts.

Row 6:
* P1, K1; rep from * across.

Row 7:
* K1, P1; rep from * across.

Row 8:
Rep Row 7.

Row 9:
Inc; work in patt to last st; inc—50 (50, 54, 54) sts.

Rows 10 through 12:
Work in patt across.

Continue to work in patt, inc one st at each end of every 4th row 3 (8, 12, 19) times more, and every 6th row 15 (12, 9, 4) times. At end of last row—86 (90, 96, 100) sts.

Work even (without inc) in patt until sleeve measures 18³⁄₄" (19¹⁄₄", 18³⁄₄", 18¹⁄₂") from cast-on edge, ending by working a right side row.

Bind off.

Finishing

Step 1:
Following Kitchener Stitch Instructions on page 55, weave ends of neck band together.

Step 2:
With right sides together, sew edge of neck band to back neck edge. Fold neck band in half to wrong side and loosely sew.

Step 3:
Referring to diagram, sew sleeves to body.

Step 4:
Sew sleeve and side seams.

November

Mini Plaid Jacket

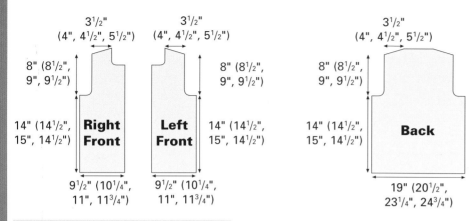

3¹/₂" (4", 4¹/₂", 5¹/₂") · 3¹/₂" (4", 4¹/₂", 5¹/₂")

8" (8¹/₂", 9", 9¹/₂")

14" (14¹/₂", 15", 14¹/₂") **Right Front** **Left Front** 14" (14¹/₂", 15", 14¹/₂")

9¹/₂" (10¹/₄", 11", 11³/₄") · 9¹/₂" (10¹/₄", 11", 11³/₄")

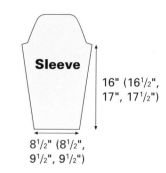

3¹/₂" (4", 4¹/₂", 5¹/₂")

8" (8¹/₂", 9", 9¹/₂")

14" (14¹/₂", 15", 14¹/₂") **Back**

19" (20¹/₂", 23¹/₄", 24³/₄")

Sleeve

16" (16¹/₂", 17", 17¹/₂")

8¹/₂" (8¹/₂", 9¹/₂", 9¹/₂")

All measurements are approximate.

Sizes:
Small   Medium   Large   X-Large

Body Chest Measurement:
32"   36"   40"   44"

Garment Chest Measurement:
39"   42"   46¹/₄"   49¹/₄"

Note: *Instructions are written for size small; changes for larger sizes are in parentheses.*

Materials:
Lion Brand Imagine, Fisherman #099, Rose #139 and Pine #173
For Size Small: 4 skeins Fisherman, 2 skeins each Rose and Pine
For Size Medium: 4 skeins Fisherman, 2 skeins each Rose and Pine
For Size Large: 5 skeins Fisherman, 3 skeins each Rose and Pine
For Size X-large: 6 skeins Fisherman, 3 skeins each Rose and Pine
Size 9 (5.25mm) straight knitting needles, or size required for gauge
Size 7 (4.5mm) knitting needles
Size 7 (4.5mm) 24" circular knitting needle
Markers
Seven buttons, ⁷/₈"-diameter
Sewing needle and matching thread

Gauge:
In stockinette stitch (knit one row, purl one row):
5 sts = 1"

Special Abbreviation

Slip, Slip, Knit (SSK):
Slip next 2 sts, one at a time, as to knit (**Fig 1**); insert left-hand needle through both sts from left to right (**Fig 2**); K2 tog—SSK made.

Fig 1

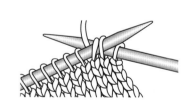

Fig 2

Instructions

Back

Edging:
With smaller size straight needles and Fisherman, cast on 95 (103, 111, 119) sts.

Rows 1 *(right side)* ***through 8:***
Knit.

Change to larger size needles.

Body:
Row 1 *(right side):*
With Rose, K3; * sl next st as to knit, K3; rep from * across.

Row 2:
P3; * with yarn in front, sl next st as to purl, P3; rep from * across.

Rows 3 and 4:
With Fisherman, knit.

Rows 5 and 6:
With Pine, rep Rows 1 and 2.

Rows 7 and 8:
With Fisherman, knit.

Rep Rows 1 through 8 until piece measures about 14" (14¹/₂", 15", 14¹/₂") from cast-on edge, ending by working a wrong side row.

Armhole Shaping:

Row 1 *(right side):*
Bind off 5 sts; work in patt across.

Row 2:
Rep Row 1—85 (93, 101, 109) sts.

Row 3:
Bind off 2 (2, 4, 4) sts; rep from * across.

Row 4:
Rep Row 3—81 (89, 93, 101) sts.

Row 5:
K1, K2 tog; work in patt to last 3 sts; SSK (see Special Abbreviations); K1—79 (87, 91, 99) sts.

continued on page 48

Mini Plaid Jacket

Row 6:
P1, P2 tog tbl; work in patt to last 3 sts; P2 tog; P1—77 (85, 89, 97) sts.

Rows 7 through 10 (12, 12, 10):
Rep Rows 5 and 6 twice (3, 3, 2) times more. At end of last row—69 (73, 77, 89) sts.

For Sizes Small and X-Large Only:

Row 11:
Rep Row 5—67 (87) sts.

Continue with For All Sizes below.

For Sizes Medium and Large Only:

Continue with For All Sizes below.

For All Sizes:

Work even (without dec) in patt until piece measures about 22" (23", 24", 24") from cast-on edge, ending by working a wrong side row.

Shoulder Shaping:

Row 1 (right side):
Bind off 4 (5, 5, 6) sts; work in patt across—63 (68, 72, 81) sts.

Rows 2 through 6:
Rep Row 1. At end of Row 6—43 (43, 47, 51) sts.

Row 7:
Bind off 5 (5, 7, 9) sts; work in patt across.

Row 8:
Rep Row 7—33 (33, 33, 33) sts.

Bind off rem sts.

Left Front

With smaller size straight needles and Fisherman, cast on 47 (51, 55, 59) sts.

Work same as Back until piece measures same as back to Armhole Shaping.

Armhole Shaping:

Row 1 (right side):
Bind off 5 sts; work in patt across—42 (46, 50, 54) sts.

Row 2:
Work in patt across.

Row 3:
Bind off 2 (2, 4, 4) sts; work in patt across—40 (44, 46, 50) sts.

Row 4:
Work in patt across.

Row 5:
K1, K2 tog; work in patt across—39 (43, 45, 49) sts.

Row 6:
Work in patt to last 3 sts; P2 tog; P1—38 (42, 44, 48) sts.

Rows 7 through 10 (12, 12, 10):
Rep rows 5 and 6 twice (3, 3, 2) times more. At end of last row—34 (36, 38, 44) sts.

For Sizes Small and X-Large Only:

Row 11:
Rep Row 5—33 (43) sts.

Continue with For All Sizes below.

For Sizes Medium and Large Only:

Continue with For All Sizes below.

For All Sizes:

Work even (without dec) in patt until you have 12 rows less than Back to Shoulder Shaping.

Neck Shaping:

Row 1 (right side):
Work in patt across.

Row 2:
Bind off 6 sts; work in patt across—27 (30, 32, 37) sts.

Row 3:
Rep Row 1.

Row 4:
Bind off 4 sts; work in patt across—23 (26, 28, 33) sts.

Row 5:
Rep Row 1.

Row 6:
Bind off 2 sts; work in patt across—21 (24, 26, 31) sts.

Row 7:
Work in patt to last 3 sts; SSK; K1—20 (23, 25, 30) sts.

Row 8:
P1, P2 tog tbl; work in patt across—19 (22, 24, 29) sts.

Row 9:
Rep Row 7—18 (21, 23, 28) sts.

Row 10:
Work in patt across.

Rows 11 and 12:
Rep Rows 9 and 10. At end of Row 12—17 (20, 22, 27) sts.

Shoulder Shaping:

Row 1 (right side):
Bind off 4 (5, 5, 6) sts; work in patt across—13 (15, 17, 21) sts.

Row 2:
Work in patt across.

Rows 3 through 6:
Rep Rows 1 and 2 twice more. At end of Row 6—5 (5, 7, 9) sts.

Bind off rem sts.

Right Front

With smaller size straight needles and Fisherman, cast on 47 (51, 55, 59) sts. Work same as Back to Armhole Shaping.

Armhole Shaping:

Row 1 (right side):
Work in patt across.

Row 2:
Bind off 5 sts; work in patt across—42 (46, 50, 54) sts.

Row 3:
Work in patt across.

Row 4:
Bind off 2 (2, 4, 4) sts; work in patt across—40 (44, 46, 50) sts.

Row 5:
Work in patt to last 3 sts; SSK (see Special Abbreviation on page 46); K1—39 (43, 45, 49) sts.

Row 6:
P1, P2 tog tbl; work in patt across—38 (42, 44, 48) sts.

Rows 7 through 10 (12, 12, 10):
Rep Rows 5 and 6 twice (3, 3, 2) times more. At end of last row—34 (36, 38, 44) sts.

For Sizes Small and X-Large Only:

Row 11:
Rep Row 5—33 (43) sts.
Continue with For All Sizes below.

For Sizes Medium and Large Only:

Continue with For All Sizes below.

For All Sizes:

Work even (without dec) in patt until you have 12 rows less than Back to Shoulder Shaping.

Neck Shaping:

Row 1 (right side):
Bind off 6 sts; work in patt across—27 (30, 32, 37) sts.

Row 2:
Work in patt across.

Row 3:
Bind off 4 sts; work in patt across—
23 (26, 28, 33) sts.

Row 4:
Rep Row 2.

Row 5:
Bind off 2 sts; work in patt across—
21 (24, 26, 31) sts.

Row 6:
Rep Row 2.

Row 7:
K1, K2 tog; work in patt across—20
(23, 25, 30) sts.

Row 8:
Work in patt to last 3 sts; P2 tog;
P1—19 (22, 24, 29) sts.

Row 9:
Rep Row 7—18 (21, 23,
28) sts.

Row 10:
Rep Row 2.

Rows 11 and 12:
Rep Rows 9 and 10.
At end of Row 12—
17 (20, 22, 27) sts.

Shoulder Shaping:

Row 1 *(right side):*
Work in patt across.

Row 2:
Bind off 4 (5, 5, 6) sts; work in
patt across—13 (15, 17,
21) sts.

Rows 3 through 6:
Rep Rows 1 and 2 twice more—5 (5,
7, 9) sts.

Bind off rem sts.

Sleeve (make 2)

Edging:
With smaller size straight needles and
Fisherman, cast on 43 (43, 47, 47) sts.

Rows 1 *(right side)* **through 6:**
Knit.

Change to larger size needles.

Body:

For Size Small Only:

Row 1 *(right side):*
With Rose, K3; * sl next st as to knit,
K3; rep from * across.

Row 2:
P3; * with yarn in front, sl next st as to
purl, P3; rep from * across.

Rows 3 and 4:
With Fisherman, knit.

Rows 5 and 6:
With Pine, rep Rows 1 and 2.

Rows 7 and 8:
With Fisherman, knit.

Row 9:
Rep Row 1.

Row 10:
Inc (knit in front and back of next st);
P2; * with yarn in front, sl next st as to
purl, P3; rep from * 8 times more; with
yarn in front, sl next st as to purl, P2,
inc—45 sts.

Rows 11 and 12:
With Fisherman, knit.

Row 13:
With Pine, K4; * sl next st as to knit,
K3; rep from * 9 times more; K1.

Row 14:
P4; * with yarn in front, sl next st as to
purl, P3; rep from * 9 times more; P1.

Rows 15 and 16:
With Fisherman, knit.

Row 17:
With Rose, K4; * sl next st as to knit,
K3; rep from * 9 times more; K1.

Row 18:
P4; * sl next st as to purl, P3; rep from
* 9 times more; P1.

Row 19:
With Fisherman, knit.

continued on page 50

Mini Plaid Jacket

Row 20:
With Pine, inc; P3; * with yarn in front, sl next st as to purl, P3; rep from * 9 times more; inc—47 sts.

Continue in patt, inc one st at each end every 10th row nine times more. At end of last row—65 sts.

Work even (without inc) until sleeve measures about 16" from cast-on edge, ending by working a wrong side row.

Continue with Cap Shaping.

For Sizes Medium and Large Only:

Row 1 (right side):
With Rose, K3; * sl next st, K3; rep from * across.

Row 2:
P3; * with yarn in front, sl next st, P3; rep from * across.

Rows 3 and 4:
With Fisherman, knit.

Rows 5 and 6:
With Pine, rep Rows 1 and 2.

Row 7:
With Fisherman, knit.

Row 8:
Inc (knit in front and back of next st); K41 (45); inc—45 (49) sts.

Row 9:
With Rose, K4; * sl next st as to knit, K3; rep from * 9 (10) times more; K1.

Row 10:
P4; * with yarn in front, sl next st as to purl, P3; rep from * 9 (10) times more; P1.

Rows 11 and 12:
With Fisherman, knit.

Rows 13 and 14:
With Pine, rep Rows 9 and 10.

Row 15:
With Fisherman, knit.

Row 16:
Inc; K43 (47); inc—47 (51) sts.

Continue in patt, inc one st each end every 8th row 10 (8) times. At end of last row—67 (67) sts.

Continue in patt, inc one st at each end every 10th row 2 (4) times. At end of last row—71 (75) sts.

Work even (without inc) until sleeve measures about 16½" (17") from cast-on edge, ending by working a wrong side row.

Continue with Cap Shaping.

For Size X-Large Only:

Row 1 (right side):
With Rose, K3; * sl next st, K3; rep from * across.

Row 2:
P3; * with yarn in front, sl next st, P3; rep from * across.

Rows 3 and 4:
With Fisherman, knit.

Row 5:
With Pine, rep Row 1.

Row 6:
Inc (knit in front and back of next st); P2; * with yarn in front, sl next st as to purl, P3; rep from * 9 times more; with yarn in front, sl next st as to purl, P2, inc—49 sts.

Rows 7 and 8:
With Fisherman, knit.

Row 9:
With Rose, K4; * sl next st as to knit, K3; rep from * 10 times more; K1.

Row 10:
P4; * with yarn in front, sl next st as to purl, P3; rep from * 10 times more; P1.

Row 11:
With Fisherman, knit.

Row 12:
Inc; K47; inc—51 sts.

Work in patt, inc one st at each end every 6th row 4 times more. At end of last row—59 sts.

Continue to work in patt, inc one st at each end every 8th row 11 times. At end of last row—81 sts.

Work even (without inc) in patt until sleeve measures about 17½", ending by working a wrong side row.

Continue with Cap Shaping.

Cap Shaping:

For Size Small Only:

Row 1:
Bind off 5 sts; work in patt across—60 sts.

Row 2:
Rep Row 1—55 sts.

Rows 3 and 4:
Work in patt across.

Row 5:
K1, K2 tog; work in patt to last 3 sts; SSK (see Special Abbreviations on page 46); K1—53 sts.

Rows 6 through 8:
Work in patt across.

Row 9:
Rep Row 5—51 sts.

Rows 10 through 12:
Work in patt across.

Rows 13 through 24:
Rep Rows 9 through 12 three times more. At end of Row 24—45 sts.

Row 25:
K1, K2 tog; work in patt to last 3 sts; SSK; K1—43 sts.

Row 26:
Work in patt across.

Rows 27 through 40:
Rep Rows 25 and 26 seven times more. At end of Row 40—29 sts.

Row 41:
Bind off 2 sts; work in patt across—27 sts.

Rows 42 through 44:
Rep Row 41. At end of Row 44—21 sts.

Bind off.

For Sizes Medium and Large Only:

Row 1:
Bind off 5 sts; work in patt across—66 (70) sts.

Row 2:
Rep Row 1—61 (65) sts.

Rows 3 and 4:
Work in patt across.

Row 5:
K1, K2 tog; work in patt to last 3 sts; SSK (see Special Abbreviations on page 46); K1—59 (63) sts.

Rows 6 through 8:
Work in patt across.

Row 9:
Rep Row 5—57 (61) sts.

Rows 10 through 12:
Work in patt across.

Rows 13 through 16:
Rep Rows 9 through 12 once more. At end of Row 16—55 (59) sts.

Row 25:
K1, K2 tog; work in patt to last 3 sts; SSK; K1—53 (57) sts.

Row 26:
Work in patt across.

Rows 27 through 50:
Rep Rows 25 and 26 twelve times more. At end of Row 50—29 (33) sts.

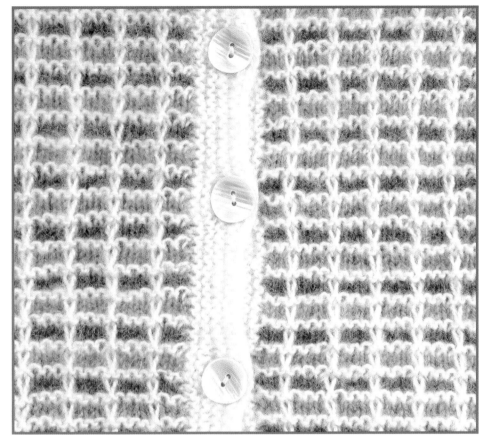

Row 1 *(right side):*
Hold jacket with right side of right front facing you. With smaller size straight needles and Fisherman, beg at lower edge, pick up and knit 103 (107, 111, 111) sts evenly spaced along center front edge.

Rows 2 through 4:
Knit.

Row 5:
Knit to first marker; bind off 3 sts; * knit to next marker; bind off 3 sts; rep from * 5 times more; knit rem sts.

Row 6:
Knit to first bound-off st; cast on 3 sts; * knit to next bound-off st; cast on 3 sts; rep from * 5 times more; knit rem sts.

Rows 7 and 8:
Knit.

Bind off.

Collar
Hold jacket with right side facing you. With smaller size circular needle and Fisherman, pick up and knit 70 sts along neck edge, beg and ending at center front.

Row 1 *(wrong side):*
Knit.

Rows 2 *(right side)* **through 7:**
Rep Row 1.

Row 8:
K34; inc (knit in front and back of next st); K35.

Rep Rows 1 through 8 three times more—74 sts.

Change to larger size needles.

Rep Row 1 until collar measures 3" from beg, ending by working a wrong side row.

Bind off loosely.

Finishing
Step 1:
Sew sleeves to body.

Step 2:
Sew sleeve and side seams.

Step 3:
Sew buttons opposite buttonholes.

Row 51:
Bind off 2 sts; work in patt across—27 (31) sts.

Rows 52 through 54:
Rep Row 51. At end of Row 54—21 (25) sts.

Bind off.

For Size X-Large Only:

Row 1:
Bind off 5 sts; work in patt across—76 sts.

Row 2:
Rep Row 1—71 sts.

Row 5:
K1, K2 tog; work in patt to last 3 sts; SSK (see Special Abbreviations on page 46); K1—69 sts.

Rows 6 through 8:
Work in patt across.

Row 9:
Rep Row 5—67 sts.

Row 10:
Work in patt across.

Rows 11 through 44:
Rep Rows 9 and 10 sixteen times more. At end of Row 44—35 sts.

Row 45:
Bind off 2 sts; work in patt across—33 sts.

Rows 46 through 48:
Rep Row 45. At end of Row 48—27 sts.

Bind off.

Sew shoulder seams.

Button Band:
Row 1 *(right side):*
Hold jacket with right side of left front facing you. With smaller size straight needles and Fisherman, beg at neck shaping, pick up and knit 103 (107, 111, 111) sts evenly spaced along center front edge.

Rows 2 through 8:
Knit.

Bind off.

Buttonhole Band:
Place markers for seven buttonholes evenly spaced along right front, having first marker 1/2" from lower edge and last marker 1/2" from neck.

Casual Rugby Pullover

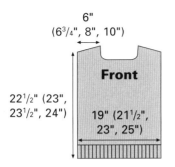

6"
(6³/₄", 8", 10")

Front

22¹/₂" (23",
23¹/₂", 24")

19" (21¹/₂",
23", 25")

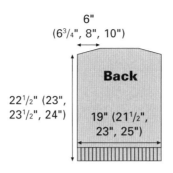

6"
(6³/₄", 8", 10")

Back

22¹/₂" (23",
23¹/₂", 24")

19" (21¹/₂",
23", 25")

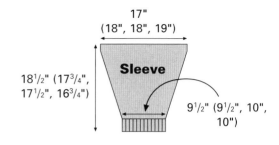

17"
(18", 18", 19")

Sleeve

18¹/₂" (17³/₄",
17¹/₂", 16³/₄")

9¹/₂" (9¹/₂", 10",
10")

All measurements are approximate.

Sizes:
Small   Medium   Large   X-Large

Body Chest Measurement:
34"   36"   40"   42"

Garment Chest Measurement:
38"   43"   46"   50"

Note: Instructions are written for size small; changes for larger sizes are in parentheses.

Materials:
Lion Brand Homespun, Ebony #313, Deco #309 and Antique #307
For Size Small: 3 skeins Ebony, 1 skein each Deco and Antique
For Size Medium: 3¹/₂ skeins Ebony, 1 skein each Deco and Antique
For Size Large: 4 skeins Ebony, 1 skein each Deco and Antique
For Size X-Large: 4¹/₂ skeins Ebony, 1 skein each Deco and Antique
Size 10 (6mm) knitting needles, or size required for gauge
Size 9 (5.5mm) knitting needles
Size 9 (5.5mm) 16" circular knitting needle
Markers

Gauge:
With larger size needles in stockinette stitch (knit one row, purl one row):
3 sts = 1"

Special Abbreviation:

Slip, Slip, Knit (SSK):
Slip next 2 sts, one at a time, as to knit (**Fig 1**); insert left-hand needle through both sts from left to right (**Fig 2**); K2 tog—SSK made.

Fig 1

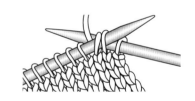

Fig 2

Instructions

Back

Ribbing:
With smaller size needles and Deco, cast on 57 (65, 69, 75) sts. Change to Ebony.

Row 1 (right side):
K1; * P1, K1; rep from * across.

Row 2:
P1; * K1, P1; rep from * across.

Rep Rows 1 and 2 until ribbing measures about 2¹/₂" from cast-on edge, ending by working a wrong side row.

Change to larger size needles.

Body:
Row 1 (right side):
Knit.

Row 2:
Purl.

Rep Rows 1 and 2 until piece measures 12" (13", 14", 15") from cast-on edge, ending by working a wrong side row.

Stripe Pattern:
Rows 1 through 20:
Rep Rows 1 and 2 of body in following color sequence:
4 rows Deco
2 rows Ebony
8 rows Antique
2 rows Ebony
4 rows Deco

With Ebony, rep Rows 1 and 2 until piece measures about 22" (23", 23¹/₂", 24") from cast-on edge, ending by working a wrong side row.

continued on page 54

December

Casual Rugby Pullover

Shoulder Shaping:

Row 1:
Bind off 6 (7, 8, 9) sts; knit across.

Row 2:
Bind off 6 (7, 8, 9) sts; purl across—
45 (51, 53, 57) sts.

Rows 3 and 4:
Rep Rows 1 and 2. At end of Row
4—33 (37, 37, 39) sts.

Row 5:
Bind off 6 (8, 8, 9) sts; knit across.

Row 6:
Bind off 6 (8, 8, 9) sts; purl across—
21 (21, 21, 21) sts.

Bind off.

Front

Work same as for Back until piece has
10 less rows than Back to Shoulder
Shaping.

Neck Shaping:

Row 1:
K23 (27, 29, 32); join second skein of
yarn; bind off next 11 sts; knit rem sts.

Note: Work across both shoulders
at same time with separate skeins.

Row 2:
Purl.

Row 3:
For left shoulder, knit across; for right
shoulder, bind off next 2 sts; knit
across.

Row 4:
For right shoulder, purl across; for left
shoulder, bind off 2 sts; purl across—
21 (25, 27, 30) sts on each shoulder.

Row 5:
For left shoulder, knit across; for right
shoulder, bind off 2 sts; knit across.

Row 6:
For right shoulder, purl across; for left
shoulder, bind off 2 sts; purl across—
19 (23, 25, 28) sts on each shoulder.

Row 7:
For right shoulder, K16 (20, 22, 25),
K2 tog; K1; for left shoulder, K1, SSK
(see Special Abbrieviation on page
52); K16 (20, 22, 25)—18 (22, 24,
27) sts on each shoulder.

Row 8:
Purl.

Row 9:
Knit.

Row 10:
Purl.

Shoulder Shaping:

Row 1:
Bind off 6 (7, 8, 9) sts; knit across.

Row 2:
Bind off 6 (7, 8, 9) sts; purl across—
12 (15, 16, 18) sts on each shoulder.

Rows 3 and 4:
Rep Rows 1 and 2. At end of Row 4—
6 (8, 8, 9) sts on each shoulder.

Row 5:
For left shoulder, bind off rem 6 (8, 8,
9) sts; on right shoulder, knit across.

Row 6:
For right shoulder, bind off rem sts.

Sleeve (make 2)

Ribbing:
With smaller size needles and Deco,
cast on 27 (27, 29, 29) sts. Change
to Ebony.

Row 1 (right side):
K1; * P1, K1; rep from * across.

Row 2:
P1; * K1, P1; rep from * across.

Rep Rows 1 and 2 until piece measures
2¹/₂" from cast-on edge.

Change to larger size needles.

Body:

Row 1 (right side):
Inc (knit in front and back of next st);
knit to last st; inc—29 (29, 31, 31) sts.

Row 2:
Purl.

Row 3:
Knit.

Row 4:
Purl.

Rows 5 through 16 (44, 36, 56):
Rep Rows 1 through 4 three (10, 8, 13)
times more. At end of last row—35 (49,
47, 57) sts.

**Rows 17 (45, 37, 57) and 18
(46, 38, 58):**
Rep Rows 3 and 4.

For Sizes Small, Medium, and Large Only:

Continue in patt, inc one st at each side
of every 6th row 8 (3, 4) times. At end
of last row—51 (55, 55) sts.

Continue with For All Sizes.

For Size X-Large Only:

Continue with For All Sizes.

For All Sizes:

Rep Rows 3 and 4 until sleeve measures 18¹/₂" (17³/₄", 17¹/₂", 16³/₄") from
cast-on edge, ending by working a
wrong side row.

Bind off.

Sew shoulder seams.

Neck Ribbing
Hold sweater with right side facing you
and right shoulder at top; with circular
needle and Ebony, pick up and knit
50 (52, 52, 54) sts evenly spaced
around neckline.

Rnd 1:
* K1, P1; rep from * around.

Rep Rnd 1 until ribbing measures 1"
from cast-on edge. Change to Deco.

Bind off loosely in ribbing.

Finishing

Step 1:
Place markers 8¹/₂" (9", 9", 9¹/₂") from
shoulder seam on front and back;
sew sleeves to body between markers
matching center of last row of sleeves
to shoulder seams.

Step 2:
Sew sleeve and side seams.

Kitchener Stitch Instructions

To weave the edges together and form an unbroken line of stockinette stitch, slip right shoulder stitches from stitch holder onto one needle and left shoulder stitches from stitch holder onto second needle-one behind the other with wrong sides together.

Thread yarn into tapestry needle; work from right to left as follows:

Step 1:
Insert tapestry needle into the first stitch on the front needle as to purl **(Fig 1)**. Draw yarn through stitch, leaving stitch on knitting needle.

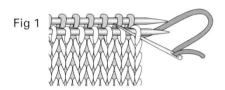

Fig 1

Step 2:
Insert tapestry needle into the first stitch on the back needle as to purl **(Fig 2)**. Draw yarn through stitch, slipping stitch off knitting needle.

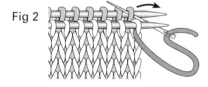

Fig 2

Step 3:
Insert tapestry needle into the next stitch on same (back) needle as to knit **(Fig 3)**. Draw yarn through stitch, leaving stitch on knitting needle.

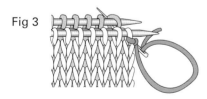

Fig 3

Step 4:
Insert tapestry needle into first stitch on the front needle as to knit **(Fig 4)**. Draw yarn through stitch, slipping stitch off knitting needle

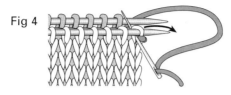

Fig 4

Step 5:
Insert tapestry needle into next stitch on same (front) needle as to purl **(Fig 5)**. Draw yarn through stitch, leaving stitch on knitting needle.

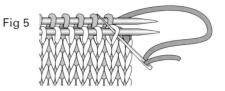

Fig 5

Repeat Steps 2 through 5 until one stitch is left on each needle. Repeat Step 2, then Step 4.

Hint: When weaving, do not pull yarn too tight or leave too loose; woven stitches should be the same size as adjacent knitted stitches.

Metric Conversion Charts

INCHES INTO MILLIMETERS & CENTIMETERS (Rounded off slightly)

inches	mm	cm	inches	cm	inches	cm	inches	cm
1/8	3		5	12.5	21	53.5	38	96.5
1/4	6		5 1/2	14	22	56	39	99
3/8	10	1	6	15	23	58.5	40	101.5
1/2	13	1.3	7	18	24	61	41	104
5/8	15	1.5	8	20.5	25	63.5	42	106.5
3/4	20	2	9	23	26	66	43	109
7/8	22	2.2	10	25.5	27	68.5	44	112
1	25	2.5	11	28	28	71	45	114.5
1 1/4	32	3.2	12	30.5	29	73.5	46	117
1 1/2	38	3.8	13	33	30	76	47	119.5
1 3/4	45	4.5	14	35.5	31	79	48	122
2	50	5	15	38	32	81.5	49	124.5
2 1/2	65	6.5	16	40.5	33	84	50	127
3	75	7.5	17	43	34	86.5		
3 1/2	90	9	18	46	35	89		
4	100	10	19	48.5	36	91.5		
4 1/2	115	11.5	20	51	37	94		

mm - millimeter   cm - centimeter

CROCHET HOOKS CONVERSION CHART

U.S.	1/B	2/C	3/D	4/E	5/F	6/G	8/H	9/I	10/J	10 1/2/K	N
Continental-mm	2.25	2.75	3.25	3.5	3.75	4.25	5	5.5	6	6.5	9.0

KNITTING NEEDLES CONVERSION CHART

U.S.	0	1	2	3	4	5	6	7	8	9	10	10 1/2	11	13	15
Metric(mm)	2	2 1/4	2 3/4	3 1/8	3 1/2	3 3/4	4 1/4	4 1/2	5	5 1/4	5 3/4	6 1/2	8	9	10

Abbreviations and Symbols

beg	begin(ning)	patt	pattern
BL(s)	back loop(s)	prev	previous
CCB	cable cross back	rem	remain(ing)
CCF	cable cross front	rep	repeat(ing)
CB	cable back	rnd(s)	round(s)
CF	cable front	sk	skip
C4B	cable four back	sl	slip
C4F	cable four front	sl st(s)	slip stitch(es)
CTB	cable twist back	sp(s)	space(s)
CTF	cable twist front	SSK	slip, slip, knit
dec	decrease(ing)	SSP	slip, slip, purl
FL(s)	front loop(s)	st(s)	stitch(es)
gm(s)	gram(s)	tbl	through back loop(s)
inc	increase(ing)	tog	together
K	knit	yd(s)	yard(s)
lp(s)	loop(s)	YO	yarn over
P	purl		
PSSO	pass slip stitch over		
P2SSO	pass 2 slipped stitches over		

* An asterisk is used to mark the beginning of a portion of instructions that will be worked more than once; thus, "rep from * twice more" means after working the instructions once, repeat the instructions following the asterisk twice more (3 times in all).

— The number after a long dash at the end of a row indicates the number of stitches you should have when the row has been completed.

( ) Parentheses are used to enclose instructions that should be worked the exact number of times specified immediately following the parentheses, such as "(K2, P2) twice."

( ) Parentheses are also used to provide additional information to clarify instructions.

Yarn Over

When working a YO after a knit stitch and before a purl stitch, bring yarn forward, completely around the needle, and forward again to complete the stitch.

A Word About Gauge

Please take the time to work a stitch gauge swatch about 4" x 4". Measure the swatch. If the number of stitches and rows are fewer than indicated under "Gauge" in the pattern, your needles are too large. Try another swatch with smaller size needles. If the number of stitches and rows are more than indicated under "Gauge" in the pattern, your needles are too small. Try another swatch with larger size needles.

A Word About Yarns

We've chosen to knit our sweaters in a variety of interesting types, textures and exciting colors of Lion Brand yarns. Any yarn that works to the same gauge may be substituted.

Terms

Right Side of the garment means the side that will be seen when it is worn.

Wrong Side of the garment means the side that will be inside when it is worn.

Right Front means the part of the garment that will be worn on the right front.

Left Front means the part of the garment that will be worn on the left front.

Continue in Pattern is usually used in a pattern stitch, and this means to continue following the pattern stitch as it is already set up (established) on the needle, working any subsequent increases or decreases (ususally worked at the beginning or end of a row) in such a way that the established pattern remains the same.

Work Even means to continue to work the pattern as established, without working any increases or decreases.